PASSAGES

..

EXPLORATIONS

OF THE

CONTEMPORARY

CITY

..

D1472538

PASSAGES

..

EXPLORATIONS
OF THE
CONTEMPORARY
CITY

..

© 2004 Graham Livesey
Published by the University of Calgary Press
2500 University Drive NW, Calgary, Alberta, Canada T2N 1N4
www.uofcpress.com

Library and Archives Canada Cataloguing in Publication

Livesey, Graham, 1960-
Passages : explorations of the contemporary city / Graham Livesey.

Includes bibliographical references.
ISBN 1-55238-141-2

1. City planning--Philosophy. I. Title.

NA9095.L58 2004   711'.4   C2004-905289-6

We acknowledge the financial support of the Government of Canada
through the Book Publishing Industry Development Program (BPIDP),
the Alberta Foundation for the Arts and the Alberta Lottery Fund—
Community Initiatives Program for our publishing activities.

Printed and bound in Canada by AGMV Marquis
∞ This book is printed on acid-free paper
Cover design, page design and typesetting by Mieka West
this page: Montreal, 1985, Graham Livesey

CONTENTS

ACKNOWLEDGMENTS

I would like to thank the following for their support and input during the development of these essays: Dr. Alberto Pérez-Gómez (McGill University), Dr. Mark Dorrian (University of Edinburgh), Dr. Morny Joy (University of Calgary), Dr. Iain Boyd Whyte (University of Edinburgh), Dr. Harry Vandervlist (University of Calgary), David A. Down (Calgary), Gregory Elgstrand (Calgary), *Avenue* Magazine (Calgary), *In Situ* Architecture Journal (University of Calgary), Andrew King (Calgary), the organizers of various ACSA Conferences, the staff of the University of Calgary Press, Lois Livesey (Victoria), Catherine Hamel and Aidan Hamel Livesey.

Financial support was generously provided by the Faculty of Environmental Design (University of Calgary) and by an anonymous gift to the University of Calgary Press.

Essay 1: An earlier version of this essay was presented at the ACSA SE Region Conference, UNC Charlotte, College of Architecture, Charlotte, North Carolina, October 26–29, 2000.

Essay 3: An earlier version of this essay was published in Morny Joy, ed., *Paul Ricoeur and Narrative: Context and Contestation* (Calgary: University of Calgary Press, 1997).

Essay 5: An earlier version of this essay was presented at the ACSA West Region Conference, Los Angeles, January 24–26, 1997.

Essay 6: An earlier version of this essay was presented at the ACSA International Conference, Copenhagen, Denmark, May 25–29, 1996.

Essay 8: An earlier version of this essay was presented at the ACSA West Central Region Conference Washington University, St. Louis, Missouri, October 2–4, 1998.

INTRODUCTION

> The city as we imagine it, the soft city of illusion,
> myth, aspiration, nightmare, is as real, maybe more
> real, than the hard city one can locate on maps, in
> statistics, in monographs on urban sociology and
> demography and architecture.[1]

An examination of the various meanings attached to the
word "passage," found in the *Oxford English Dictionary*,
reveals a set of interrelated definitions that have direct
relevance to an exploration of contemporary urban structures. According to the dictionary a passage is that "by
which a person or thing passes or may pass; a way, road,
path, route, channel; a mountain pass; an entrance or
exit."[2] This noun definition is admirably complemented
by the verb form of the word, which states that passage
is the "action of passing; going or moving onward, across
or past; movement from one place or point to another, or
over or through a space or medium; transition, transit."[3]
Therefore, the word "passage" unites both an action
of movement with the constructed entity; it is the defined linear space through which people, products, and

information may pass. Appropriately, the word also refers to a portion of a text or speech.

The following comprises eight interrelated essays that explore a series of topics as they relate to the contemporary city. They examine the global urban landscapes that have emerged since the Second World War. Sprawling cities, such as San José (California) or Calgary (Alberta), are defined by unbounded low-density development that is traversed by freeways, flight paths, and communications networks connecting elsewhere; traditional urban structures are virtually absent. The dominance of modernist space has radically challenged the role of architecture in the global city. The first two essays examine these fundamental topics. The next group of three studies linguistic structures (narrative, metaphor, and gesture) that define and express the contemporary city and which are necessary for recording, describing, and communicating. The final group of writings looks at formal structures (points, lines, and surfaces) that comprise a city and contain an enormous amount of knowledge and potential. Each essay presents background material on the topic and moves toward one or a number of pertinent ideas about the topic and its relationship to the city. A montage of ideas are presented that attempt to describe aspects of the operation of contemporary cities; in no way is this intended to be an exhaustive or detailed study.

The essays are largely theoretical, and in most cases do not provide extensive historic examples or background.

The outlook of these writings has evolved from the pessimistic to the cautiously optimistic, from rejecting the landscapes of the contemporary city to examining them on their own terms. The intent of these writings is to strive for a greater understanding of the environments we build and inhabit. The essays are informed by the work of a number of key writers. In the first case are those who have addressed the contemporary city specifically, including Kevin Lynch, Robert Venturi, Richard Sennett, and Albert Pope. In the second case are a number of thinkers, primarily philosophers, who explore material that has been important to specific topics. These include Michel Butor, Paul Ricoeur, Henri Lefebvre, and Michel de Certeau. While there has been something of a shifting evolution in the essays, there has also been a concerted effort to seek linkages between the topics. Finally, I employ the historic periods of the premodern, modern, and postmodern throughout the text. Each of these periods has its own operational logic,[4] and each is present to one degree or another in contemporary cities.

Contemporary cities cannot be taken for granted; they are complex and rapidly evolving entities. Our understanding of urban environments must continually be challenged as part of an ongoing process of interpretation.

Chicago, 1981, Graham Livesey

1 SPACE: the HETEROTOPIC DIMENSION

Many have written about the seemingly chaotic and incoherent evolution of contemporary cities, of the endless development and lack of connection between structure and inhabitation. When one examines urban growth during the last several decades it is evident that traditionally recognizable urban spaces, forms, and elements have given way to a more complex and elusive interplay of spaces, constructions, and technologies; in other words a new type of urban development has emerged. In particular, changes to urban space, and its definition, have had enormous impact on how cities are evolving. Henri Lefebvre affirms that we are "confronted by an indefinite multitude of spaces;"[1] or, new systems of space that remain little understood. Michel Foucault argues that we are in the age "of the simultaneous, of juxtaposition, the near and the far, the side by side and the scattered."[2] The spatial forces generated by global economic and communications systems have altered the spatial textures of the city to produce "heterotopolis."

Beyond the larger forces that have shaped the city over the last several decades, there has emerged an active involvement in the evolution of the city by numerous new disciplines and grassroots constituencies. The proliferation of voices during the postmodern era is a vital aspect of contemporary society. As a result we see a multitude of different languages of space engaged in trying to shape and define the contemporary city. Some of these include: geography, sociology, community activism, feminism, environmentalism, ethnic and economic subcultures, architecture, planning, transportation engineering, and land development. Each discipline and constituency understands and describes urban space differently, often generating conflicting interpretations. Finding a common ground between all the factions involved in contemporary urban development is difficult. These differing spatial models provide a very real heterotopic condition as spatial structures vie with one another or are superimposed on each other. In his book *The Production of Space*, Lefebvre searches for a unitary spatial language that will give coherence to the analysis of space. He organizes his study of space into: space as perceived (social practice); space as conceived (representations of space); space as lived (representational space); and the history of space (both abstract and absolute). In this brief exploration of the spatial aspects of the contemporary city this order will be reversed, beginning with a brief history of urban space, leading to notions of representational and social space.

::

Prior to the twentieth century, urban space was understood as a negative condition that arose between structured elements; space was an invisible medium that was not often considered as a material dimension. Nevertheless, urban spaces were shaped by the form of the city, resulting in coherent types of space such as the square, the street, and the boulevard. Early in the twentieth century traditional notions of space were destroyed by the new cosmology of Einsteinian physics and technological advances in production, transportation, and communications. While physicists contemplated the spatial structure of the universe and space-time continuities, artists and designers attempted to translate the new theories of space into practice. Inspired by these developments in physics and art, the notion of space emerged as a tangible aspect of design.[3]

These changes in understanding led to the spatial explorations of early modernism, reflected in the experiments of Cubism, Futurism, de Stijl, and Constructivism. Reyner Banham has succinctly described the orthodox early modernist conception of space as infinite and homogeneous, measured by an invisible system or structure of coordinates, and having a particular emphasis placed on motion, either by the observer or implied by the structure.[4] Simultaneously, developments in construction technology in the nineteenth century led to structure being separated from the definition of space.[5] The architecture and urbanism of the early modern movement may consequently be described as a series of tectonic elements aligned with a Cartesian system of coordinates that attempted to manifest the infinity of space. Modernist space presented a new universal sense of space in which architecture appeared as free-standing and disconnected. Subsequently, this concept of space invaded the city, inverting the traditional relationship between space and urban form.

Despite the notion that space could be conceived as infinite and homogeneous, during this period architects and urbanists (particularly the European avant-garde movements) [6] for the first time treated space as the material or reality of architecture and urban design. This shift in emphasis is also evident in the emphasis on function over the formal aspects of architecture. Modernist preoccupations with space began to have dramatic effect at the urban scale in the post-Second World War era, resulting in what is commonly understood as global urban sprawl, or the rise of suburban forms of development. Robert Venturi, Denise Scott Brown, and Steven Izenour have defined this condition as follows:

> The space of urban sprawl is not enclosed and directed as in traditional cities. Rather, it is open and indeterminate, identified by points in space and patterns on the ground; these are two-dimensional or sculptural symbols in space rather than buildings

in space, complex configurations that are graphic or representational.[7]

The contemporary city reflects this condition with a plethora of new and often little-understood spaces that "overwhelm the architectural gesture, [and] ultimately dominate the contemporary urban environment. Vast parking lots, continuous or sporadic zones of urban decay, undeveloped or razed parcels, huge public parks, corporate plazas, high speed roads and urban expressways, the now requisite *cordon sanitaire* surrounding office parks, industrial parks, theme parks, malls and subdivisions...."[8] These are some of the new spatial types or conditions that define contemporary urbanism and which are of a different nature from the Cartesian space that defined modernism. These are spaces that architects and planners tend to design thoughtlessly or ignore as forms of urban blight.

The predominance of space paradoxically, developed at the same time that the structure of the city changed from an open to a closed system. Albert Pope notes that the open and continuous structure of the original nineteenth-century gridiron has imploded into the closed and fragmented city, what he describes as the city of "ladders." Pope defines a ladder as the "remainder of a partially eroded grid,"[9] or a closed fragment of urban structure. The ladder is a useful structural notion that describes the disintegration of the contemporary city into an endless system of disconnected enclaves reflected in the organization of much of suburbia. The dominance of space has emerged at the same time as the fragmentation of the city, further adding to the heterotopic nature of the urban realm.

The sprawling city that emerged coincidentally with the communications revolution can be described as a complex system of spaces randomly interrupted by urban stuff (buildings, signs, infrastructure, etc.). It is zoned as a closed system by the transportation and infrastructure patterning of the horizontal surfaces, and by the regulatory systems that seem to guide its evolution. Urban space is made sensible by rules and signs that direct movement and action. This notion is affirmed by Susan Sontag when she writes that "space is black, teeming with possibilities, positions, intersections, passages, detours, U-turns, dead-ends, one-way streets...."[10] Venturi et al. determined this when examining Las Vegas in the early 1970s in their seminal study, *Learning From Las Vegas*. The realization that space was dominated by two-dimensional signage systems that directed traffic and unabashedly sold pleasure relegated architecture to a secondary role in the definition of urban space.

Surfaces have supplanted both the materiality of architecture and the phenomenology of space. The abstract nature of the contemporary city, described by Venturi and Sontag, means the reduction of space to a two-dimensional visual field organized by a multitude of systems. As Lefebvre suggests, there has been a flattening of space and the emergence of quasi-spatial dimensions:

> Thus space appears solely in its reduced forms. *Volume* leaves the field to *surface*, and any overall view surrenders to visual signals spaced out along fixed trajectories already laid down in the 'plan.' An extraordinary – indeed unthinkable, impossible – confusion gradually arises between space and surface, with the latter determining a spatial abstraction which it endows with a half-imaginary, half-real physical experience. This abstract space eventually becomes the simulacrum of a full space (of that space which was formerly full in nature and in history).[11]

The building as billboard continues to be a reality in the contemporary city, despite a renewed nostalgia for the materiality of traditional architecture reflected in the promotion of tectonics and "craft." In the contemporary city the exterior skin of a building remains a critical dimension of architecture, the possibilities of coherently exploring space being mainly an interior condition. The innovation of twentieth-century architecture and urbanism has been the materialization of space and the consequent dematerialization of architecture. This arises, as Frederic Jameson states, from a disjunction between the human body and the city.[12] The technological extensions of the body, mechanically and electronically, have created this disjunction. The human body has been extended to the point where the body and the immediacy of urban environments have been largely negated.

The contemporary urban condition requires strategies of engagement; it is futile to assume that the structure of the contemporary city will disappear or can be reconstructed as a false reproduction of the past. Through our human inventiveness we must make the potential in space come alive. Despite the scale of contemporary urban space, the closed structures on the ground, its constantly shifting boundaries, and the necessity for an endless signage system to render it comprehensible, the hermeneutical role of architecture persists, as does the need to develop ways of finding locations in space. We are in and of space; it is a fundamental condition of our existence. We search for a spatial project against the world in which we find ourselves. In a pluralistic urban heterotopia spatial figures are constantly being made, then sustained, altered, or dismantled. Defined space is a fleeting condition that has more to do with action than with form. Urban space is many things: constructed, commodified, experienced, demolished, designed, and/or narrated. Urban space is a project or an artifice; infinite territories to be engaged, altered, and/or lived. Space is "a set of relations between things."[13] Despite the seeming incoherence of the spaces we construct, either consciously or by default, there are strategies that are and can be employed to populate, transform, and question the spaces of sprawl. As Lefebvre and Michel de Certeau have argued, space is a social construct within which we exist, in which we act.

According to Lefebvre, social space encompasses things and actions. Social space is the "outcome of past actions, social space is what permits fresh actions to occur, while suggesting others, while prohibiting yet others."[14] Therefore, space is an active condition to be engaged. Lefebvre writes that "each body *is* space and *has* its space: it produces itself in space and it also produces that space."[15] A heterotopic spatial condition can be inhabited by using a multitude of methods:

> Every space is already in place before the appearance in it of actors.... This pre-existence of space conditions the subject's presence, action and discourse, his competence and performance; yet the subject's presence, action and discourse, at the same time as they presuppose this space, also negate it.[16]

Michel de Certeau proposes that "space is a practiced place."[17] He writes that space "occurs as the effect produced by the operations that orient it, situate it, temporalize it, and make it function in a polyvalent unity of conflictual programs or contractual proximities."[18] The body turns otherwise undefined space into comprehensible spaces, as a project, an act of making or territorializing. This occurs as both an individual and a collective activity. Routes, boundaries, abodes, intersections, and spaces are established both individually and collectively, fleetingly and in a more enduring way, that reinforce the heterotopic condition. Space is thus able to depict many states of being: emotional, linguistic, cultural, economic, and/or ideological. The city remains a tapestry of ever-changing spaces, juxtaposed, and overlapped, in which no space "ever vanishes utterly, leaving no trace."[19]

::

We must acknowledge that space often exists in dimensions beyond those understood by architects, planners, and urban designers. The practice of regulatory agencies and established professions does not necessarily coincide with social space, or everyday practice. Engineers determine the stratification or fragmentation of urban space in the first order, setting out the systems that allow for the movement of traffic, products, information, waste, energy, water, and the like. This, together with a complex regulatory bureaucracy, zones the spaces according to use; this method, much maligned in recent years, is necessary to coordinate the scale and toxicity of the environment. All of this is subservient to the basic commodification of land that underscores capitalism. It is no wonder that there is no coherence or human scale, in a traditional sense, to the resulting spaces. This merely provides a substructure for all the groups and disciplines who will attempt to inhabit the city. As noted earlier, space is fragmented between disciplines, each of which has its own language that particularizes and problematizes space. The spatial coherence of the past has given way to the fragmented pluralism of postmodernism.

Pope argues that we have collectively failed to understand the true nature of the changes to the city, knowledge of which would substantially alter our strategies for urban design. In particular, he stresses that applying formal models from the past will not do anything to contribute to or change the new urban spaces that surround the vestiges of the nineteenth-century gridiron city. Often hidden from the eyes of the professional, unable to see beyond formalistic models that they project into an unreceptive milieu, are a wide range of strategies for engaging the space of the post-industrial city, in particular those developed by urban subcultures. As Lefebvre and de Certeau argue, urban spaces are rendered habitable through the strategies of popular culture. For example, the "power centre," a disparate collective of large retail structures in a parking lot, becomes a new urban paradigm whose spatial structures seem to defy traditional classification. If one reverts to the agora, the forum, the piazza, and the boulevard as models, it will remain incomprehensible. Nevertheless, despite the paucity of design inherent in these environments, they are actively used by suburbanites who do manage to make sense of the structures.

Spaces come into existence and survive or disappear. While the combination of modernity and contemporary technology and economics has produced space as the dominant dimension in the structure of the city, this is fragmented space that results from the practices of zoning, transportation engineering, and land speculation. It may read as an endless space that defies definition by singular projects and is impenetrable to the phenomenology of experience; however, spatially the city is more about distinctions between scales of traffic engineering and land zoned as residential, commercial, institutional, or industrial. Any actual mixing of these causes an inordinate strain in the system as planners, engineers, politicians, and community groups struggle with hybridization. However, as Foucault notes, this is the power of the heterotopic approach: "heterotopia has the power of juxtaposing in a single real place different spaces and locations that are incompatible with each other."[20]

Within the world of professional urban design there has been a sustained critique of the modernist city since the 1950s. There has been the work of the various neo-traditionalist movements, including proponents of the European city (Aldo Rossi, Leon and Robert Krier, Maurice Culot, Vittorio Gregotti et al.) and small-town America (Peter Calthorpe, Andres Duany, Elizabeth Plater-Zyberk et al). There is, however, an alternate stream of thinking, less pessimistic about modernism, led by Rem Koolhaas and others (including MVRDV, Neutelings and Riedijk and Foreign Office Architects), that is tackling the forces that are rapidly shaping cities across the world. By invoking various modernist and postmodernist movements, this group, centred in Europe, is producing provocative work. Other architects and urbanists are responding imaginatively to the challenges provided by the contemporary city. These have included Steven Holl, Bernard Tschumi, and Will Alsop. These designers are developing strategies for inhabiting the spaces of the contemporary city: deconstructing the rules, building new reference systems, searching for new architectural typologies, or establishing a choreography of events.

The production of heterotopic space requires working through the seeming homogeneity and closed nature of the contemporary urban structures. The emphasis on surface found in cities can be challenged by relocating depth in the urban experience. The plethora of languages involved in defining the systems of spaces that comprise the post-industrial city must be seen as the basis for the continuing evolution of the city as an ongoing project. Urban space emerges from a conglomerate of strategies. While the space of the contemporary city is homogeneous in appearance, it has resulted from and can be inhabited by heterogeneous processes.

Montreal, 1987, Graham Livesey

2 BUILDINGS: the ANOMALOUS CONDITION

> When circumstances defy order, order should bend or break: anomalies and uncertainties give validity to architecture.[1]

The role of architecture in contemporary cities has been controversial during the last several decades. Many believe that contemporary architecture has been rendered immaterial, reduced to signage and surface, particularly in urban situations, and that a return to traditional values and models is the most appropriate strategy for architects to adopt. This is a nostalgic position that tends to negate the developments of twentieth-century architecture and the evolving nature of contemporary cities. Nevertheless, the strategies that architects should adopt in the contemporary city are not always obvious. Does architecture affirm a status quo condition, or does it present alternative visions? In this essay I wish to examine one such strategy, the development of anomalous or atypical structures.

According to the dictionary an anomaly is a "deviation from rule, type or form; irregularity."[2] To be anomalous is to be exceptional or abnormal. In the historic city one could argue that the anomalous buildings were often the institutions (churches, town halls, prisons, etc.) or landmark structures that stood out from the housing that made up the vast majority of a city's fabric. This idea still carries through today in contemporary cities, where elements, not necessarily monumental, rupture the order of the structure. These are the singular structures of the city; however, not all singular structures are unconventional or deviant, nor do they necessarily break rules. In the case of the anomalous we are looking at structures that defy the common order.

In his discussion of the "conventional element," in *Complexity and Contradiction in Architecture*, Robert Venturi explores the ramifications of breaking established orders:

> A valid order accommodates the circumstantial contradictions of a complex reality. It accommodates as well as imposes. It thereby admits "control *and* spontaneity," "correctness *and* ease – improvisation within the whole. It tolerates qualifications and compromise ... [The architect] does not ignore or exclude inconsistencies of program or structure within the order."[3]

This description of an accommodating order shows how the contemporary city should or could operate; the order of the city must accommodate the complexities of contemporary living. Venturi further writes, "Meaning can be enhanced by breaking the order; the exception points to the rule. A building with no 'imperfect' part can have no perfect part, because contrast supports meaning.... Order must exist before it can be broken."[4] As Venturi acknowledges, anomalies affirm and challenge the general condition. There is a role for deviant elements, or structures, in the order of the city; a city is enhanced by those structures, monumental or not, that break the rules, that are nonconforming and even subversive.

As an example of this approach, the work of Le Corbusier demonstrates how an order can be interpreted and intentionally challenged. John Summerson has written the following: "... a building by Le Corbusier is a ruthless dismemberment of the building *programme* and a reconstitution on a plane where the unexpected always, unfailingly, happens.... He sees the reverse logic of every situation. He sees that what appears absurd is perhaps only more profoundly true than what appears to make sense. His architecture is full of a glorious, exciting contrariness...."[5] One technique that Le Corbusier employed was to play anomalous elements against an established ordering system. He also, as Summerson notes, generated new typologies by inverting traditional assumptions about building elements and relationships; he explored new forms and materials in his work. It is out of this "contrariness" that meaning in Le Corbusier's work emerges, along with its striking influence. A project such as his Salvation Army Building in Paris (1929–33) is radically different from its surroundings, and is sited in a way that breaks with traditional rules for urban buildings. Yet, it is a building whose difference reveals much about how relationships between a building and a context may be defined.

The anomalous condition, whether structural or spatial, creates a condition of difference. Jacques Derrida writes: *"Différance* is the systematic play of differences, of traces of differences, of the spacing [*espacement*] by which elements relate to one another."[6] According to Jonathan Culler the concept of *différance* defined by Derrida contains three meanings:

1) The universal system of differences, spacings, and distinctions between things; attention paid not to a vocabulary itself but to the dimensions along which items in a vocabulary separate themselves from each other and give rise to each other;

2) The process of *deferral*, of passing along, giving over or postponing; of suspension, pro-traction, waiving, and so on; a 'spacing' in time; and

3) the sense of *differing*, that is, of disagreeing, dissenting, even dissembling.[7]

The first and third aspects of Culler's definition are of particular interest here. Inherent to Derrida's concept of *différance* is the spacing between, in this case between a normal and an abnormal condition, a condition where the spacing becomes more defined than it does between like elements. The "universal system of differences" gives individual elements their definition. The notion of degrees of difference, from the minimal to the maximal, as suggested by Henri Lefebvre, is also a useful contribution here.[8] The anomalous strives for maximum degrees of difference, but may also function under minimal conditions. In reverse it can be stated that the norm, or the typical, gains its legitimacy against the anomalous or atypical. The third part of Culler's definition, the idea of differing, providing an alternate or dissenting position, provides a reinforcement of the ideas presented here; it recognizes the subversive nature of anomaly.

The pursuit of difference requires a close reading of existing conditions and an engagement in the responsibilities architects and others have for constructed environments. There has been a preoccupation in the last two decades with the marginal and the peripheral, a fascination, on the part of some architects, with edge and in-between conditions. This is an affirmation of Derrida's ideas, using the techniques of deconstruction to expose the fallacies and contradictions inherent in systems. Within the seemingly homogeneous spatiality of the contemporary city, anomalous elements create spatial tensions, the spaces of difference. Difference can both undermine and perpetuate existing conditions. Deconstructionist strategies can populate homogeneous space with heterogeneous conditions.

The contemporary city is often perceived as either chaotic or exceedingly banal. The banality of suburbia has to do with the lack of difference, the sameness, the proliferation of singular typologies. In the contemporary city, the norm has been severely criticized for many decades, where low density, poorly constructed and placeless development proliferates. Post-Second World War architecture rarely seems to define public space adequately. Architects tend to celebrate surface play and concentrate on the potential of interior environments. In the best case, anomalous structures can throw into question, or relief, the nature of standardized practices. They can also raise questions as to what is the order of contemporary urban development. The anomalous can address atypical conditions and generate new types or norms.

Anomalous structures can employ many strategies: they may be monstrous, parasitical, subversive, alternative, deviant, or strange. Works of architecture, landscape, infrastructure, or urban design can include inconsistencies, exceptions, circumstantial elements, distortions, contrasts, inversions, paradox, irony, mistakes, contradiction, juxtaposition, or the unconventional use of conventional elements. They may also appear to be quite conventional, incorporating only subtle abnormalities.

The work of leading "deconstructionists," including Daniel Libeskind, Peter Eisenman, Zaha Hadid, and Frank O. Gehry, provides examples of this. However, as Michael Benedikt has pointed out in his thoughtful book *Deconstructing the Kimbell*, there is a real role for the techniques of deconstruction as articulated by Derrida, and these can be employed in the reading or creation of any work. Architects as diverse as Frank Lloyd Wright and Le Corbusier incorporated formal and functional techniques that align with deconstruction. All of these architects put forward projects that question the norm, that could be said to be anomalous, that examine and challenge the formal and functional aspects of buildings.

The form of a building, which provides its linguistic dimension, can express many things; it is the metaphorical aspect of architecture. Within a given urban context a singular building is like a word or phrase in the larger urban text. It can be an undistinguished word in a sentence or the moment of disruption. The use of unusual form is an obvious way for creating a condition of difference. Landmark structures like the Eiffel Tower, Sydney Opera House, or Guggenheim Museums (New York and Bilbao) achieve iconic status due to the atypical nature of their forms; they register in the collective memory and imagination. The unusual qualities of a building (shape, size, colour, or material) can give it an anomalous dimension.

The landmark structure, either intentional or not, may disrupt the banality of contemporary cities.

Complementing form is the engagement with form, the functional intention or response. To be functionally precise is a difficult task, as function inevitably changes and evolves. The modern search for the functionally defined building has produced many disappointing results. Functional openness and ambiguity allows the form of a building to be more enduring. It also allows for shifting and evolving connections to the context. To be functionally anomalous would be to propose a building type that does not fit into contemporary zoning orthodoxy or to contain the absence of form. The radical juxtaposition of functions within a building structure can also engender anomaly, as can certain kinds of multi-functional approaches. Some structures, typically industrial buildings, are open and fluid to change. The typical suburban house, while a relatively closed structure in its organization, can accommodate a variety of living arrangements. Buildings evolve and shift functionally as they accumulate history, and through ongoing relationships with context and inhabitants.

Anomalous structures can also be structures that appear to be out of context, as either functionally or formally inappropriate to a specific location. Radical juxtaposition is one of the most powerful means for establishing difference. The nineteenth-century North American city was premised on this idea. The ground plane established a two-dimensional order. Within that order buildings were given latitude with respect to function, form, and size. This resulted in heterogeneous development as subsequent waves of development created radical juxtapositions, for example, a house adjacent to a skyscraper. In older urban areas the cacophony of structures is inherent to the structure of cities.

Contemporary urban zoning and regulatory control attempts to create homogeneity, to at least rule out what are believed to be unhealthy or undesirable functional adjacencies. Nevertheless, anomalous conditions often pre-exist or slip through the cracks: the nonconforming structure or the building that was not built according to codes or regulations. In other cases the owner and/or designers argue for a deviation from the regulations and manage to convince the approving authorities to accept an atypical solution. There are always sites, even within the most conservative developments, that are anomalous in shape, location, or servicing and which deserve a suitable response.

Searching for difference is often the striving for the shocking or the new.[9] There is the danger that anomaly becomes novelty, or an empty effort to be different just to be different. One important role of the artist or designer is to demonstrate to society alternative conditions and opportunities. Often radical movements will become consumed and subsumed by the collective culture, rendering difference null and void. Conversely, a work of difference can be an enduring work of resistance, or the presentation of an alternate view. Another inherent danger is that a radical work is either ignored or is seen as a threat that reinforces the resolve of the status quo. What may appear to many to be strange or foreign can become the target of prejudice, ridicule, or contempt. On the other hand, anomalous conditions provide spaces for the plurality of contemporary society – the many subcultures that populate contemporary cities, people of varying ethnic, religious, sexual, economic, artistic, and political orientations – to exist within. The atypical can embrace the marginal or disenfranchised.

> Differences endure or arise on the margins of the homogenized realm, either in the form of resistances or in the form of externalities (lateral, heterotopical, heterological). What is different is, to begin with, what is *excluded*: the edges of the city, shanty towns, the spaces of forbidden games, of guerrilla war, of war. Sooner or later, however, the existing centre and the forces of homogenization must seek to absorb all such differences, and they will succeed if these retain a defensive posture and no counterattack is mounted from their side. In the latter event, centrality and normality will be tested as to the limits of their power to integrate, to recuperate, or to destroy whatever has transgressed.[10]

The role of the anomalous structure, the construct that attempts to describe difference is, as Henri Lefebvre points out, a difficult and dangerous one. While the deviant has an operational logic and role, it can also be the target of prejudice, misunderstanding, or ideological opposition.

One role for artists and designers in our society is that of the avant-garde experimenter; another is the *provocateur*. To reinforce the status quo has not been the task of leading artists or architects in Western society during the last century. There is also a role for the architect to challenge norms, to strive for a better situation, not to accept ready-made solutions. This is not a wilful task, it is not searching for difference just for the sake of it. There is a danger in creating structures that are merely freakish, the targets of misunderstanding. This is not a case for the purposefully outlandish, nor is it a case for the work of artists and designers to always strive for the new. However, it is an argument for work that is provocative. Not every construction should strive to be anomalous, and yet structures that depart from the typical order provide the order with its definition. The space of difference allows a structure to be read or interpreted, to contain meaning; the forces that influence any project are responded to by the designer in any number of ways. Responding to a context to create meaningful spaces is a difficult task in the rapidly evolving environments that define the contemporary city. Setting up propositions that develop strategies based on a close reading of the situation, or searching for difference, can lead to ruptures in the fabric of the city.

In a homogeneous architectural condition, such as is found in many suburban developments, difference can be found among the inhabitants and in the vestiges of local landscape that remain. Most of which is atypical is hidden from view. The opportunities for abnormal structures are rare, and would likely be met with a hostile reaction by community groups protecting what they perceive to be the value in their neighbourhoods: stylistic and economic consistency. The addition of singular anomalous structures into such environments can also go unnoticed, absorbed by the banality of the surroundings. On the other hand, an atypical construct could initiate a debate about the nature of persistent norms. One critical and anomalous condition found in all urban environments consists of the spatial figures executed in a complex and fleeting way by the actions of the inhabitants. These actions, which are endless and complex, leave subtle traces that can challenge the presumptions of suburban development; they are the trajectories of the inhabitants.

The anomalous structure is a form of pollution, the trace of a toxic element, an infecting agent, or a virus. Unusual solutions to a problem are what provocative designers like Le Corbusier or Frank Gehry strive for: not difference for the sake of difference, but difference in order to expose or reveal some idea, condition, or experience. Projects that incorporate unusual or unexpected functions or arrangements can produce new typologies that respond to new situations. Juxtaposition does not always result in conflict; eventually an intermediate zone emerges. The buffer zone, employed in a widespread manner in contemporary cities, is the mandated space of difference. Meaning arises from a "system of differences."[11] Cities need unusual and atypical conditions. This adds to the complexity of the urban environment. Difference provides meaning, or the means for interpreting structures, creating the space of difference. Anomalous buildings and spaces provide the city with unique landmarks, large and small, and make the city memorable. These structures provide anchoring points in the city. The idea that urban structures should conform to some commonly held notion of tradition is a conservative attitude toward urban development that denies the forces shaping contemporary cities. The "neo-traditionalist" approach argues for typological consistency by employing historically developed models. Cities are complicated, inclusive and messy; they must support a panoply of approaches, ideas, and opportunities. The order of cities must be complex enough to embrace diversity, or what some people might understand as deviance. The inhabitants of cities are increasingly diverse; therefore, the heterogeneity of urban structures becomes a necessity.

Montreal, 1986, Graham Livesey

3 NARRATIVE: the HEURISTIC JOURNEY

This essay will explore potential linkages between narrative theory, which emanates primarily from literature and philosophy, and contemporary architecture and urbanism to gain a greater understanding of the reciprocal relationship between human actions and design. Paul Ricoeur, a leading authority on narrative, points out that "life has to do with narration."[1] A narrative may be defined as a structured sequence of events configured by a plot; narratives are stories. Narrative modes include myths, novels, biographies, histories, gossip, and dreams. The constitutive element of a narrative is an event, a significant occurrence that can contribute to the formation of a plot. Emplotment is the creative act of drawing events together into a narrative. Our lives, individually and collectively, are defined by narrative structures. Architecture and cities can be understood as works of human making, which are designed, constructed, inhabited and interpreted. Ultimately, architecture and cities shape spaces in which human actions unfold. Narrative theory contributes to understanding these unfoldings.

Ricoeur states in the preface to the first volume of *Time and Narrative* that "whereas metaphorical description reigns in the field of sensory, emotional, aesthetic, and axiological values, which make the world a habitable world, the mimetic function of plots [or narrative] takes place by preference in the field of action and its temporal values."[2] In his earlier text, *The Rule of Metaphor*, Ricoeur explores metaphor in rhetorical, structural, and hermeneutical terms, moving from the figural aspects of metaphor contained in a discussion of Aristotle to the existential implications of metaphor and the "the power to 'redescribe' reality."[3] It is with metaphor that architecture and cities are more typically associated. Ricoeur's work on narrative primarily addresses questions of time with reference to discourse and texts. In his writings there is little discussion of the world or those human works that contribute to the shaping of the world.

In *Time and Narrative* Paul Ricoeur presents his theory of emplotment, based largely on a reading of Aristotle's *Poetics* and Augustine's *Confessions*. In the text he introduces the notion that the work of a poet is to make plots. To imitate human actions, to make a plot is "to make the intelligible spring from the accidental, the universal from the singular, the necessary or the probable from the episodic."[4] Ricoeur also introduces the core of his monumental exploration of narrative and time, his notion of a "threefold" understanding of mimesis in which the idea of figuration is fundamental.

The first part of the model Ricoeur labels mimesis$_1$; he writes that the "composition of the plot is grounded in a pre-understanding of the world of action, its meaningful structures, its symbolic resources, and its temporal character."[5] This refers to the practical world of everyday action, which Ricoeur describes as the realm in which stories or narratives are prefigured. Narratives are based on actions that have motives, agents, and take place in the world and in time. As Ricoeur implies, architecture and spatiality can be considered as part of the world that prefigures narratives, as both meaningful structure and as symbolic systems. This pre-narrative condition is affirmed when he writes that "literature would be incomprehensible if it did not give a configuration to what was already a figure in human action."[6] This statement, which concludes his discussion of the prefigurational aspect of narrative, confirms that action is figural and points forward to his discussion of the second, and central, part of his model.

Mimesis$_2$, the configurational aspect of Ricoeur's theory of emplotment, functions in three ways. Firstly, it mediates between individual events and a story or narrative as a whole; it gives shape to a succession of events. Secondly, "emplotment brings together factors as heterogeneous as agents, goals, means, interactions, circumstances, unexpected results."[7] Thirdly, it unites the temporal characteristics of the plot. The configurational role of emplotment is the "grasping together" of heterogeneous factors into a meaningful story that possesses shape (or figure) and a "sense of ending." In Ricoeur's model this is the action of the poet, and also the aspect that coincides most closely with other forms of creative production such as design.

Mimesis$_3$ completes the circular nature of the model and "marks the intersection of the world of the text and the world of the hearer or reader."[8] This third part of the model is the interpretative aspect, which reaffirms Ricoeur's ongoing exploration of hermeneutics and the "conflict of interpretations." We, as readers, gain understanding of our lives and of our world by engaging in what a work (text, artifact, building, or city) reveals; that which is prefigured and configured is refigured. The act of interpretation reveals worlds that might be inhabited and contributes to our inhabitation of the material world. This does not apply only to reading, but also to our physical engagement with the world.

Anthony Paul Kerby sums up Ricoeur's model of emplotment and his use of various modes of figuration in the following:

> Emplotment, in histories and fictions, takes a prefigured world of events and actions and draws out or proposes a configuration that serves to organize worldly events into meaningful sequences and purposes. This textual structure is in turn the mediating cause of the reader refiguring his or her own world in light of the possibilities offered by experiencing the world of the text [work].[9]

Many of the ideas alluded to above are suggested in a quotation by the British architect Nigel Coates, who describes the use of various narrative strategies in the design of a large urban project for the Isle of Dogs area of London:

> The first [narrative] is drawn out of the place itself – its barren landscapes, broken buildings and empty docks. Then a video narrative, explores the possible mixing up of work and home without ever referring to buildings directly. Thirdly, each piece of the island ... develops its own industrial process to mark a narrative of movement, process and sequence. The final narrative occurs when the experience of the place – living on the island, riding the bus, settling into the work/home landscape – puts all these layers together.[10]

Coates' description closely matches the mimetic model employed by Ricoeur as the architect gives shape to form based on an interpretation of the context and by creating narratives. From this comes a potential for the emergence of new, unforeseen, narratives. I would like to briefly extend Ricoeur's three stages of mimesis: prefiguration, configuration, and refiguration. The cyclical and continuous nature of the model presents a vital and timely way of considering human creativity and production.

::

When an architect or urban designer is asked to design a project, usually by a client, the practical world of everyday action shapes, to one degree or another, the project that will emerge. Design takes place within a dense cultural context, or web of constraints, which determines methods of construction, uses of space, symbolic systems, economic parameters, and languages of architecture. For an architect this world is also shaped by already existing structures that define the site or context. The design of a building, and its subsequent inhabitation, are also pre-determined to a degree by program (the design brief or functional requirements), the budget, legal restrictions, building practices, and numerous other factors and forces. This coincides with Ricoeur's proposition that the world is prefigured by narrative, that stories are latent in the world and that narration and life are intertwined. It can be suggested that architecture and cities are both part of and emerge from a prefigured world.

In a series of essays that examine the role and structure of novels, the French writer Michel Butor affirms the ideas that Ricoeur has examined philosophically. He explores narrative structure, temporal discontinuities, space, and the role of the book. Butor argues that the novel is the "laboratory of narrative,"[11] and he suggests that all novels are about journeys in time and space. He utilizes the idea of the "trajectory" as a description for narrative structure or plot and unites this with notions of space, both architectural and urban.[12] The trajectory is a "temporal movement through space";[13] it is a line drawn in space, a figure, or a narrative. This notion is similar to the central role of "figure" in Ricoeur's model. Butor, like Ricoeur, is also interested in the relationship between the text and the reader, or a union of trajectories. In a departure from Ricoeur's linear definition of narrative structures, Butor posits the notion of narrative webs or networks. He writes that narration "is no longer a line, but a surface on which we isolate a certain number of lines, of points, or of remarkable groupings."[14] Butor notes that contemporary space differs from traditionally defined space in that locations in space are networked together in more complicated ways. He writes that every site "is the focal point of a horizon of other sites, the point of origin of a series of possible routes passing through other more or less determined regions."[15] This affirms the vitality of Ricoeur's model and the prefigured nature of narratives, and that complex environments, like cities, are defined by narratives. Beyond the interconnection of all points in an environment or territory, there is also the notion put forward by Butor that narrative trajectories are distorted or shaped by objects or structures, such as architecture, that define and modify space.[16]

The configurational aspect that is proposed in the second part of Ricoeur's model is also vital, as it is the intentional shaping of, or giving of structure to, the narrative. This is akin to the process undertaken by architects in the design and execution of a work of architecture (both in drawings and in actual construction), or by urban designers considering a project. Normally this is a collective activity that takes some time to accomplish. The giving of architectural form or structure to a disparate range of elements and requirements is like Ricoeur's description of narrative emplotment. Out of this heterogeneous wealth of factors a project emerges, or is "grasped" together: the poetic act of the "productive imagination." The events (meetings, decisions, and discoveries) that configure the design of a project have a structure in time very similar to Ricoeur's notion of emplotment. It is a grasping together of the significant events or decisions into a comprehensible work; it is the poetic act.

Peter G. Rowe, in his book *Design Thinking*, has used accounts of design projects by a number of architects as one form of evidence for understanding the workings of design. He maintains that the design process "assumes a distinctly episodic structure, which we might characterize as a series of skirmishes with various aspects of the problem at hand."[17] Rowe is describing a process analogous to Ricoeur's notions of configuration as described in the second part of his mimetic model. A figure gradually emerges out of what may begin as a random series of events or episodes. This is not necessarily a linear, sequential, or continuous activity, but usually has a structure based on the prefigured context. However, Ricoeur's model challenges the primacy of originality within creative acts, firmly re-establishing that making is part of a historical and cultural context; creativity is to a large extent an interpretation of that which is given, or prefigured.

The third part of Ricoeur's mimetic model addresses what happens to a work when it is given to the world to be read, interpreted, or inhabited. Examining the relationship between the world of a work and that of a reader, Ricoeur proposes that "hermeneutics takes hold of the hinge between the (internal) configuration of a work and the (external) refiguration of a life."[18] Architecture and urban design, like any other creative work, contain an intentional world that emerges from that which is prefigured (given) and that which is configured (the poetic act). All works participate in this "fusion of horizons" that occurs between the world of the work and the world of the reader or inhabitant. The relationship between building and inhabiting is reciprocal as architecture exists as part of the context which prefigures narrative and architecture itself.

Michel de Certeau has provocatively described how the actions of those living in cities (or buildings) create narratives; in particular, he has written about the activities of those who walk in urban spaces:

> In the technocratically constructed, written, and functionalized space in which the consumers move about, their trajectories form unforeseeable sentences, partly unreadable paths across a space.[19]

De Certeau also describes the disjunction that can arise between a text and a reader, and between a user and space, what he describes as "indeterminate trajectories" which do not "cohere with the constructed, written, and prefabricated space through which they move."[20] He extends the narrative model into ways of inhabiting space when he argues that it is the paths and patterns of movement in and through a space that define that space.[21] The act of walking is like speech; it is a narrative strategy. This appropriates space, it acts out the space, and it defines relations among "differentiated positions"[22] in a manner similar to those defined by Ricoeur and Butor.

Through spatial and narrative engagement architectural and urban spaces are defined; some spaces are activated, others are negated. This is an evolving condition that often does not correspond with the intentions of the designer.[23] Thus, any space, geometric, technical, or bureaucratic, is rendered human through time and action. These alternative or subversive readings allude to Ricoeur's "conflict of interpretations," or the multiplicity of interpretations any work can produce. These readings can come often from the languages and actions of the disenfranchised or dispossessed. The techniques of inhabitation employed by overlooked subcultures can provide renewal to seemingly abandoned or hopeless environments. De Certeau shows how the narrative structures prescribed by urban designers, engineers, and planning authorities are often appropriated by the users or inhabitants (consumers) to their own ends, producing counter or alternative narratives.

Human actions trace out figures or trajectories, series of movements that can be comprehended, reinforcing the notion that "each human life traces out a complex figure that necessarily intersects and interacts with the figures of others."[24] This statement affirms that our movements or journeys in the world, and in time, are figural and carry the latent potential, through intersections with other figures, for contributing to a plot. The patterns, or figures, we make in space and time as we inhabit the world are potentially metaphorical and narrative. A figurative intersection occurs between a figural definition of space, as determined by architecture, and the figural actions of human engagement with the world.

::

Architecture and cities exist in time, as do narratives; therefore, interpretations will necessarily alter over time and according to who undertakes the reading. A work, whether a building or text, is subject to changing interpretations. The pervasiveness of narratives is not immediately evident to architects and urban designers. Architects do, on occasion, engage the prefigured aspects of narrative in their work, but normally revert to architectural means (drawing, models, and construction) to execute the configurational aspects of design. The refigurative aspects of design are not as carefully studied by architects and urban designers as they should be. Nevertheless, the relationship between narrative processes and design has been explored by a number of contemporary architects and urban designers who have focused on the event – the constitutive element of a narrative – and the correlation between movements and spaces. Noteworthy examples include Aldo Rossi, Nigel Coates, Bernard Tschumi, Rem Koolhaas, John Hedjuk, and Peter Eisenman.

There is much in Ricoeur's "threefold" mimetic model that lends itself to a renewed understanding of the design and inhabitation of buildings. The figurative, as Ricoeur suggests, is prefigured in our symbolic systems, the multiplicity of languages that we comprehend, configured by our productive or poetic tendencies and refigured through interpretation and inhabitation. The figural qualities of form and human action, and their relationship to the spatial world and narrative, are vital sources of thinking for architects. The question remains as to what is the nature of the figures or trajectories being described, whether the references are abstract, anthropomorphic, mechanistic, textual, or informational.

While Ricoeur falls short of stating that we write our own life stories, he affirms that narrative is essential to our human existence in time and space. I would suggest that architects tend to concentrate on the configurational aspects of design, neglecting a rigorous exploration of that which is prefigured and how their work allows for refiguration. By using Ricoeur's discussion of metaphor as figural discourse and the figurational aspects of em-plotment in the structuring of human narratives, it can be concluded that design is both metaphorical and participates in narrative. Architecture and cities figure the spaces in which we dwell or move. Our actions trace figures that can be retold in the narrative ordering of our life stories. Intersections between humans and their world, between each other and with ourselves, create the events that plot our journeys in time and space. Narrative engagements with architecture and cities also include the distortion of trajectories by objects and events, and the subversive strategies described by Michel de Certeau.

Fredericton, 1978, Graham Livesey

4 METAPHOR: the NEED for INNOVATION

> Not only language but the whole of intellectual life
> is based on a play of transpositions, a play of sym-
> bols, which can be described as metaphorical. Then
> again, knowledge always proceeds by comparison, so
> that all known objects are connected to one another
> by relations of interdependency.[1]

The issue of poetics and meaning in contemporary
architecture and urbanism invokes, often unknowingly,
the actions of metaphor. Metaphor, from the Greek word
metaphora (*meta*: over, and *pherein*: to carry),[2] is a linguistic device that is appropriate when considering the
interpretation of artifacts. A building can be metaphorical, an object or element can be metaphorical, and cities,
in all their immense complexity, can be understood in
metaphorical terms. No doubt for some the calling up of
metaphor is a romantic notion, verging on the decorative
and ornamental. However, as Lakoff and Johnson have
demonstrated, metaphor operates at all levels of everyday
language: orientational (based on spatial orientations
derived from the human body), ontological, containing

(marking boundaries and territories), personifiable, and structural. They write that the "essence of metaphor is understanding and experiencing one kind of thing in terms of another."[3] Most metaphors are so common in everyday use that they have lost their metaphorical power; they are examples of "dead" metaphor, or represent movement from the figurative to the literal.

Metaphor is the most fundamental form of figurative language (along with simile, synecdoche, and metonymy) and implies a transference or a turning of language toward figurative meaning. In other words, "aspects of one object are 'carried over' or transferred to another object, so that the second object is spoken of as if it were the first."[4] Metaphor has the aim of "achieving a new, wider, 'special' or more precise meaning."[5] Writers on the subject have attributed various operative qualities to metaphor. Ernst Cassirer states that metaphor is one of the "essential conditions" of speech.[6] According to Wheelwright, metaphor provides a "unique flash of insight."[7] For Paul Ricoeur, metaphor implies "semantic innovation, an emergence of meaning;"[8] or, out of linguistic discourse arise metaphors that reveal aspects of reality.[9] Like the writer or storyteller drawing together disparate events into a plot or narrative structure, metaphor, at its most powerful, is a profoundly creative act. The joining of context, creative act, and interpretation operate within the realm of metaphor as a hermeneutic enterprise. This produces both a mimetic and a heuristic condition,[10] mimetic in that creativity draws from a context, and heuristic because it exposes something new.

Each of the terms used in a metaphor implies what Nelson Goodman calls a "schema." The innovation in metaphor occurs when there is "a transfer of a schema, a migration of concepts, an alienation of categories."[11] In other words a schema is imposed on an uncongenial realm, giving rise to conceptual conflicts. Goodman describes this as a territorial invasion, an "immigrant schema" applied to a home realm.

James M. Edie sums up the operational nature of metaphorical expression in the following:

> A word is not a metaphor just because it is *used*, though this is a necessary condition; a word becomes a metaphor when it is used to refer with a new purpose, *with a new intention*, to a previously disclosed aspect of experience in order to reveal a hitherto unnamed and indistinct experience of a different kind. The metaphorical use of words thus brings about a reorganization, a refocusing of experience, which continues to grow in complexity with each further use of the word in a distinctively new sense, with each new *purpose*.[12]

Metaphors tend to operate between nouns, whether animate or inanimate; however, they can also work through adjectives and verbs, which provide a more indirect form of metaphorical expression.[13] Most powerfully, they act between nouns in various combinations of animate and inanimate couplings: "he is a beast" (animate/animate), "she is a factory" (animate/inanimate), "the city is an old woman" (inanimate/animate), "the city is paradise" (inanimate/inanimate). According to Christine Brooke-Rose, "any identification of one thing with another, any replacement of the more usual word or phrase by another, is a metaphor."[14] In design it is impossible to avoid metaphorical interpretations of work. During the heroic period of twentieth-century modernist architecture and urbanism, the language of architecture was stripped of its traditional guises and linguistic connotations, to be replaced with a new language and set of metaphorical references. The classical body was replaced by the machinery of modern industry. Today, the metaphorical context presents a multiplicity of possibilities, where new voices and metaphors continue to emerge.

::

The study of metaphor has burgeoned into a significant aspect of philosophy and literary theory, and is covered across the ideological spectrum. On one hand we find pragmatic skeptics who do not believe that metaphors operate,[15] and on the other those, including Nietzsche and Valéry, who have suggested that metaphor expresses "the very structure of reality."[16] Jacques Derrida has written on the subject, concluding that metaphors erase themselves;[17] he emphasizes the "limitless metaphoricity of metaphor."[18] Among contemporary philosophers, Paul Ricoeur has devoted a substantial amount of writing to the subject, including his text *The Rule of Metaphor*, which traces metaphorical operations through classical rhetoric, structuralist semantics, and hermeneutics. His formulations provide a useful background for studying the subject as it might pertain to the construction, inhabitation, and interpretation of cities.

Ricoeur makes a distinction between narrative and metaphor that is vital to our discussion. Whereas narrative addresses action and the temporal dimension, metaphor tends to operate in the material world of human construction; while linguistic, it is eminently about the world of things.[19] Metaphor claims to yield some truth about reality.[20] Ricoeur suggests that metaphor operates between semantics, imagination, and feeling. Examining Aristotle's definition of metaphor reveals the importance of contemplating similarities and the "picturing function," or the connection with the imagination. Another aspect is the figurative, which gives discourse the "nature of a body," making discourse appear.[21] In the rhetorical tradition of persuading and pleasing, metaphor functions by "giving appropriate names to new things, new ideas, or new experiences, or to decorate discourse...."[22] As a semantic innovation metaphor must make sense:

> The *maker* of metaphors is this craftsman with verbal skill *who*, from an inconsistent utterance for a literal interpretation, draws a significant utterance for a new interpretation which deserves to be called metaphorical because it generates the metaphor not only as deviant but as acceptable.[23]

What role does imagination play in this operation? Ricoeur suggests three steps. Firstly, "imagination is understood as the 'seeing.'"[24] This is insight which is both "a thinking and a seeing";[25] it reveals the proximity of the terms brought together in the metaphor. This results in new kinds of assimilation through seeing likeness "in spite of and through the differences."[26] Secondly, there is the pictorial or figurative dimension of imagination, or the "borderline" between the verbal and the image. Thirdly, there is what Ricoeur calls the "suspension" or "the moment of negativity brought by the image in the metaphorical process."[27] This opens up the function of reference in poetic discourse and the proposition that there is "a suspension and seemingly an abolition of the ordinary reference attached to descriptive language."[28] Here, the role of imagination is vital to the metaphorical process. In other words, poetic or metaphorical language employs a complex strategy in order to reveal the deep structures of reality. Borrowing from Goodman, Ricoeur affirms the productive aspect of metaphor suggested in the above quote discussing the making of metaphors.

Ricoeur proposes that feelings "accompany and complete imagination"[29] in the same threefold manner. He argues that the concrete nature of metaphor comes from the linking of the cognitive, imaginative, and emotional aspects of metaphor.

In other writings Ricoeur examines the innovative dimension of metaphor. In language he notes that words often mean more than one thing, and that through the operations of sentences the creative dimension of language appears. In metaphor a "semantic clash" occurs that "creates a new situation,"[30] or a new meaning. Therefore, metaphor alters our perceptions and provides new insights, expanding the operations of language. From this brief review of Ricoeur's theories of metaphor we can suggest that metaphor is powerfully useful in understanding the city.

::

A metaphorical description of a city provides a convenient way for citizens and outsiders to understand the city, which "as a whole, is inaccessible to the imagination unless it can be reduced and simplified."[31] A host of metaphors have been applied to cities throughout history. For example, metaphorically, a city "may be termed or compared with a factory, a madhouse, a frontier, a woman...."[32] The metaphorical descriptions of a city evolve with the changing history of the city;

a once-thriving city can descend into ruin, with the consequential change in expression that goes with it. Individual landmarks can provide the symbol of a city: the Eiffel tower in Paris, the Golden Gate Bridge in San Francisco, the Opera House in Sydney. The skyline of New York, famous the world over, provides a metaphorical and recognizable image of the city, one which invokes the density, energy, and magnificence of New York.

Some cities enter cultural mythology, while others do not capture the imagination; they lack striking features or qualities. The overall structure of the city has typically been constructed along symbolic or metaphorical lines; symbolic if transcendental, metaphoric if worldly. Since the emergence of cities several thousand years ago there has been a steady shift from the sacred to the secular, or from the symbolic to the metaphorical. We can distinguish three periods in the evolution of the Western city: the premodern city (cosmos/philosophy); the modern city (science/industrialism); and the postmodern city (communications technology).

Premodern cities, such as the ancient Greek or medieval city, are powerfully symbolic in that there exists strong transcendental or cosmological connections in their structure and institutions. In the late stages of the Renaissance, a preoccupation with the symbolically perfect, or ideal, city developed. However, metaphorical notions also appeared during the Renaissance: the city as a body[33] and the city as a house. The latter is to be found in Alberti's fifteenth-century text on architecture, in which he writes: "... in the City itself, so in these Particular Structures, some Parts belong to the whole Household, some Uses of a few, and others to that of a single Person"[34] and "... a House is a little City."[35]

The Industrial Revolution and the rise of capitalism brought dramatic transformations to the city. The social and technological upheavals changed both the real and the metaphorical structure of the city as urban alienation grew. The modern industrial city has been described by many in mechanistic terms. In the foreword to his book *The City of Tomorrow and its Planning*, published in 1924, Le Corbusier opens with a polemical metaphor: "A town is a tool."[36] This union of town and industrialization is consistent with other famous mechanistic metaphors employed by Le Corbusier and others in the 1920s. Like the house, the city is a machine. Le Corbusier also writes: "The street is a traffic machine; it is in reality a sort of factory for producing speed traffic."[37]

The development of endless contemporary or postmodern urbanism, enhanced by electronic technology and increasing globalization, has led to a city which is fragmented and decentralized. Metaphors drawn from contemporary technology are often employed: "force field city,"[38] or "the airport as city square."[39] In North America the suburban shopping mall is being replaced by the "power centre," a fragmented collection of large and small retail and fast food outlets surrounded by parking, a term that metaphorically describes a new typology.

::

The American writer Ralph Waldo Emerson explored re-
curring themes in his writings that addressed American
urban metaphor. M.H. Cowan traces these themes: the
frontier city, the new city, the city of God, the city of Man,
and the organic city. Each of these informs the evolution
of North American cities in the modern period and the
collective understanding of the city. The frontier remains
part of the mythology of North America, evident in the
brash expansionism of cities across the continent. The
new city often recalls or imitates a European precedent,
often plainly named after an existing European city. The
utopian religious desire to build a New Jerusalem in a
New World, to escape from persecution, underlies the
city as "The City of God." "The City of Man" describes
the classical ideal, which powerfully inspired American
politics and aesthetic culture. Finally, "The Organic
City," the city united with nature, versus the industrial
city, captures the hold that the pastoral ideal has had over
the North American city since the eighteenth century.[40]

During the nineteenth century the city evolved from
a static system into one in constant flux. The structure of
the city was radically altered by the industrial, social, and
economic revolutions of the period. The metaphor of the
magnet drawing people to the industrial cities was powerfully appropriate. The debate between the city and the
country became polarized, particularly in the English-

speaking world. In America, the Midwest became the mythical heartland of the nation, and rural virtue was pitted against what was perceived as the urban decadence of cities like New York and Chicago. The domestic and communal aspects of the provincial town were actively promoted: "... the small city can boast of home-like surroundings and friendly atmosphere, in an invidious contrast with the larger urban centers."[41] The following quotation describes, in metaphorical language, a view of the emerging industrial city that would be widely exploited in American literature of the period:

> [The city] was a Babylon, a den of iniquity, the breeding ground of sin and evil and the temptress of the good Christian. It was the home of the infidel.... It was a bloodsucker which strangled the farmer.... The city was un-American.... It robbed him of what was promised ... it stole from his children.... [42]

The large city as a melancholic and destructive environment that pits the withdrawn individual against the passionate mob and the inhuman forces of government and industry is found in Dickens, Poe, and Kafka, to name only a few authors who have explored the industrial urban world. Here many metaphorical descriptions of the city can be applied: the city as purgatory; the city as prison; the city as betrayer; the city as wasteland; the city as seductress. A famous example is Thomas Jefferson's oft-quoted remark that "cities are sores on the body politic...."[43] Inversely, the industrial city was a place of economic and cultural opportunity, a chance to escape the parochialism of the country and town. In the large cities fortunes could be made, intellect and creativity could expand, and cultures could intermingle.

> The city was the great mart not only for one's produce, but also for supplying one's consumption needs.... The city was the fabulous place.... It was the place of maximum opportunity....[44]

The North American city typically embodies notions of progress, the frontier as a noble condition, and regional distinctions. Biological metaphors also abound that deal with growth and structure. The distillation of various factors – spatial, geographic, economic, social, cultural, formal – provide the basis for a metaphorical description of a city.[45] The city of Chicago is described as a hodge-podge, an approach to growth characteristic of most American cities. Chicago is a city oscillating between "gigantic enterprise and tremendous violence."[46] Energy, drive, innovation, and progress create a "herculean business enterprise."[47]

::

The metaphors that can be applied to cities and their elements are numerous and intriguing: organic (biological, bestial, and anthropomorphic), technological (mechanical and electronic), linguistic, literary, religious, economic, political, formal, communal, and architectonic. Metaphors inform the everyday city, and the mythic or ideal cities of the imagination. Over time there has been a shift from the symbolic or transcendental to the metaphoric or immanent. Each provides meaning through transpositional linkages, one to an overriding order (e.g., cosmos), the other to a cultural or linguistic context. The shift from the stable symbolic systems of the premodern world to the endless flux of the postmodern is reflected in a symbolic evolution from the city as a body (premodern), the city as a machine (modern) to the city as an ever-shifting network or web (postmodern). The city as corrupt versus the city as an ideal will also continue to inform the interpretation and ideology of the city. Nevertheless, certain metaphorical structures have provided continuity across history: the city as a body, the city as a house, the city as a machine, and the city as a labyrinthine network. Here, these four metaphorical descriptions of the city will be briefly examined, metaphors that are historical, but which still have currency.

The city as a body, a metaphor powerfully subscribed to during the Renaissance, is still valid despite the technologies that have extended and altered the body. Elaine Scarry writes that there is a direct correlation between artifacts and the body; this suggests that the city, no matter what other dimensions govern its structure, is a bodily extension.[48] In the classically perfect body that provides the basis for the Renaissance city, portrayed by Francesco di Giorgio, we progress through the various parts of the body representing the organization of the city. The heart of the city comes to mind, and the qualities associated with the head, each carefully located. In the eighteenth century, the psychological or emotional body comes to prominence, and will play an important role in the exploration of the emerging industrial city. The body as a slave to industrialization, a product of capitalist production, is evident in the writings of Karl Marx. The networked city of the second half of the twentieth century exploits the inner workings of the human brain and nervous system, an electronic model that enables the displacement of the material city. Today, the contemporary body is defined by modern medicine, warfare (e.g., the Holocaust and Hiroshima), means of production, the media, and communications technologies.[49] Each of these provides a metaphorical link to the contemporary city.

The city as a house has also maintained a strong presence in the evolution of the Western city: the city as a place that one belongs to as a "citizen," the idea that a city provides comfort and protection. Alberti employed the metaphor, as has the late-twentieth-century architect Aldo van Eyck, who has written: "... a house must be like a small city if it is to be a real house – a city like a large house if it is to be a real city."[50] The domestic view of the city is clearly evident in the Anglo-American cultures, which place tremendous emphasis on the house, at the expense of the city. While the city as a whole is no longer house-like, the notion of domesticity is a powerful force in the shaping of suburbia.

The city as a machine emerged coincidentally with the Industrial Revolution. New technologies produced a radical redefinition of the economic role of the city, and also the very structure and internal operations of nineteenth- and twentieth-century cities. The role of infrastructure and mechanization added new dimensions to the city, notions of efficiency, mechanical imagery, and function emerged, as they did in architecture. The modernist city derived much of its design from the industrial machine as a metaphorical model. The legacy of the modern industrial city underpins the post-industrial city that has emerged in North America since the Second World War.

The image of a network, web, or force field is now often used to depict the contemporary city. By now almost meaningless through overuse, these terms describe the emphasis placed on communications, providing some structural and existential insight into the city. Many contemporary metaphors used to describe both cities and architecture are taken from the computer industry, which in turn has borrowed its terminology from other disciplines. Like all such descriptions, these metaphors can go unchallenged, providing a simplistic vision of a complex condition. Certainly there has been an etherealization of the city,[51] with less emphasis on the shape of the city. The loss of recognizable shape in urban development means that many traditional metaphors applied to the city no longer work.

::

> It is impossible to understand the human mind or human behavior except by making a metaphorical detour, not through the human body, but through the objects in the world which first polarize the human bodily activity and enable the self to experience itself as distinct from the world, by reciprocally endowing the world with human characteristics and itself with the characteristics of experienced objects in order, then, to rediscover these characteristics as its own.[52]

In the epigraph Michel Leiris defines metaphor as a transpositional play between objects, through language, that helps language to provide an interconnected context for meaning. The city cannot easily be reduced to simple metaphors; however, the well-used metaphors of the city explored above offer both a means for understanding cities and images of the city that provide existential orientation.

64

The innovative, or creative, aspect of metaphor provides new insights into the nature of cities. The role of metaphor also extends to the structure or shape of individual elements or buildings within the city. Metaphor restores imagination to the city. Within the overall structure of a city there are the numerous constructions and spaces that comprise the fabric of the city. The attachment of metaphorical meaning to an urban structure, object, or space is vital to recognizing the structure or shape of a city; "Recognition of shape is vital to the identification of cities."[53] The architect gives a building metaphorical potential, which changes or is reinterpreted over time. Metaphor asserts the reality of an object. A poet gives new life to symbols by recontextualizing them; metaphor has become the symbolic dimension in the city.

The structure of a city and the buildings, spaces, and technology that comprise this structure are latent with metaphorical description, both banal and innovative. This is the hermeneutical dimension of artifacts, the "conflict of interpretations" vital to understanding the contemporary world. The ability to give and hold metaphorical meaning is a necessary aspect of any urban structure, and it behooves planners, politicians, architects, urbanists, activists, and developers to understand this. New metaphors that describe contemporary cities provide collective insight into how cities operate and can be understood.

Montreal, 1985, Graham Livesey

5 GESTURE: the PUBLIC LANGUAGE of the BODY

It is well known that the public realm, in a traditional sense, in those cities or portions of cities that have emerged since the Second World War has been largely abandoned. Public space has been usurped by what Richard Sennett describes as "the tyrannies of intimacy."[1] Those parts of cities that retain vital public areas were generally formed prior to the emergence of the automobile as an extension of human motility. It seems nostalgic to imagine the restoration of a meaningful public realm in which significant events, both communal and individual, might take place. However, if we accept Sennett's definition that the city is "a human settlement in which strangers are likely to meet,"[2] and it is in the city that most of the world's population is to be found, then the examination of contemporary public space continues to be a vital subject. This essay explores human gesture in order to understand the potential for human interaction in contemporary cities.

The contemporary Canadian photographer Jeff Wall has referred provocatively, in a short text written on gesture, to the decline of bodily gesture, particularly in the city, during the modern era. He writes:

> The ceremoniousness, the energy, and the sensuous-
> ness of the gestures of baroque art are replaced in
> modernity by mechanistic movements, reflex ac-
> tions, involuntary, compulsive responses. Reduced
> to the level of emissions of bio-mechanical or
> bio-electronic energy, these actions are not really
> 'gestures' in the sense developed by older aesthet-
> ics. They are physically smaller than those of older
> art, more condensed, meaner, more collapsed, more
> rigid, more violent.[3]

Wall's carefully staged photographs are concerned with
the representation of the body and the significance of
the gesture frozen in the moment of enactment. In this
regard his work bears some resemblance to the long and
important career of Henri Cartier-Bresson, who also
documented a wide range of public human gestures.
Wall's exploration of the smallness of human gestural
expression is his way of revealing the nature of contemporary society, to "lift the veil a little on the objective
misery of society and the catastrophic operation of its law
of value."[4] Wall's observations are clearly evident in the
contemporary city, where a tradition of public gestural
codes has been reduced to involuntary and cryptic movements that form no coherent public language.

The declining influence of what Sennett has aptly
termed "play-acting" in the public spaces of the contemporary city has been comprehensively explored in his

important text *The Fall of Public Man*. In that work he writes that "playacting in the form of manners, conventions, and ritual gestures is the very stuff out of which public relations are formed, and from which public relations derive their emotional meaning."[5] Sennett cogently argues that the public realm of the city should be an expressive one, where the entire range of human thought and emotion is vibrantly present. Contrary to many current notions, public space was not where one expressed individuality; instead one participated in a theatrical continuity before an audience of strangers. Traditionally this was accomplished through conventionalized forms of dress, speech, and behaviour (much like acting) that corresponded to a person's gender, class, and occupation. These conventions have, for instance, been recorded in Gilbert Austin's text *Chironomia: or, A Treatise on Rhetorical Delivery*,[6] first published in 1806.

The decline of public space, particularly in North America, has occurred in the face of increased emphasis on private space and the narcissistic/egocentric tendencies of contemporary society. Ironically, in many contemporary cities, it is often among those who hold no real power over the shape of urban growth that gestural languages still have powerful meaning, often as urban codes of resistance. The gestural languages associated with African-American street cultures,[7] or the collective expression that arises during times of protest, are examples of this. Both of these themes are documented in Spike Lee's 1989 film *Do the Right Thing*, which traces cultural differences played out in a typical urban block in the Bedford-Stuyvesant district of New York City. These gestural languages of the street describe the fullness of human interaction between body and the world, much as is found in the worlds of theatre and sign language, other gestural forms of human expression.

Gestures, as significant and often symbolic (or metaphorical) movements of the body, belong to both language and space; gesture is an essential part of human communication. Gestures range from the posture assumed by the entire body, through a wide range of movements of hands and limbs, to the subtlest movements of the face. The linguistic dimensions of bodily gestures are particularly explicit in the sign languages employed by the deaf. Through the use of complex hand and arm movements, together with other facial and bodily expressions, the deaf are able to carve out a linguistic space in which the shape and locations of gestural signs create a visual language or landscape. A spatial zone around the body has been structured as a linguistic space. True sign languages employed by the deaf, as opposed to various translations from spoken and written languages, are independent languages with their own grammars, structures, and expressive potentials – complete symbolic and expressive systems that convey the full range of intellectual and emotional communication. As one might expect, sign languages such as ASL (American Sign

Language) are extremely spatial. Oliver Sacks, who has devoted a text to the subject, writes:

> The single most remarkable feature of Sign [ASL] – that which distinguishes it from all other languages and mental activities – is its unique linguistic use of space.... We see then, in Sign, at every level – lexical, grammatical, syntactic – a linguistic use of space: a use that is amazingly complex, for much of what occurs linearly, sequentially, temporally in speech, becomes simultaneous, concurrent, multi-leveled in Sign ... what looks so simple is extraordinarily complex and consists of innumerable spatial patterns nested, three-dimensionally, in each other.[8]

Sign languages employ the fullness of space and time to create narrative structures that have a cinematic virtuosity, allowing the signer to manipulate these dimensions.[9] It has been demonstrated that the deaf have a greater perceptual sense of space than do the hearing, and when describing objects or spatial conditions can employ bodily gestures to give very detailed portrayals. Sign languages arise from gesture and, thus, unlike speech, are fully embodied. From the sign languages used by both actors and the deaf we can learn about the expressive potential of the gestural body and also about the figural and linguistic dimensions of space, what may be called the "grammaticization of space."[10] The interaction between body, space, and language in theatrical performance and sign language provides relevant models for exploring the latent potential in contemporary cities for the making of architecture. Gestural languages arise from a specific cultural context, and as in all languages, the meaning of a certain action and the potential for expression is prefigured by the linguistic milieu from which it derives; against this background speech and interpretation emerge.

Those who have studied the nature of human gesture have developed classification systems for gestural communication. Wilhelm Wundt, the pioneering German psychologist, published a work in 1921, subsequently translated as *The Language of Gestures*, in which he ascribes gestures to the following categories: demonstrative, imitative (descriptive), connotative (descriptive), and symbolic. While the text is dated in many of its propositions, his system still provides a useful structure and corresponds closely with a more recent formulation found in David McNeill's *Hand and Mind: What Gestures Reveal about Thought*.[11] However, McNeill adds a group that addresses prelinguistic forms of gesture that incorporate rhythmical and punctuation types of gestures.

Demonstrative forms of gesture are the simplest and most direct. In effect, they are a pointing, toward things in the world, toward ourselves.[12] They provide an orientation to the world of others and for our body.[13]

Demonstrative gestures are immediate and concrete, reverting back to prelinguistic conditions. Therefore, they are also used to express emotions. Wundt identifies two basic concepts: "parties to a conversation" or differences between 'you' and 'I' (or self and other); and "spatial relationships" or spatial directions as they pertain to the body. Demonstrative gestures "originate in the person's own body as the center of all spatial orientation."[14] Other demonstrative gestural concepts include: dimensional qualities; parts of the body; and "gestures which place the three dimensions of space in the context of past, present, and future."[15] These qualities unite space and time. The notion of pointing, contained in these kinds of gestures, is essential to all communication and orientation in the world.

Wundt divides descriptive gestures into those that are imitative and those that are connotative. Imitative gestures are pictorial or representational, in that they replicate the form of an object. In this case an object is drawn in the air or imitated by the hands. For example, a house can be indicated by making an outline of its typical form with the index finger, and an animal can be described by hand forms that imitate its characteristic shape.[16] The gestural facility of the hands is supported by facial expressions. Connotative gestures represent objects by "singling out arbitrarily one of its secondary traits to represent it."[17] Closely related to imitative forms of gesture, the connotative form is identified by Wundt as being either transitory or held indefinitely, and can border on the symbolic.[18] Both forms of descriptive gesture fall within the realm of metaphor, hence they give an innovative and poetic dimension to gestural languages.

Wundt describes symbolic gestures as the final and broadest category, in which a sign invokes a "mental concept." As opposed to the directness of demonstrative and descriptive forms of gesture, symbolic forms operate through association, giving languages abstract and poetic dimensions. Symbolic gestures operate like spoken languages and other symbolic structures, in that they are deliberately created and must be learned; they belong to a shared understanding.

Public space, in all forms, is a product of human making in that it is tangible and cultural; therefore, it corresponds to the human body. It responds to human needs, metaphorically replicates aspects of the human body and contributes to making the world animate in human terms.[19] In the modern era, urban space was increasingly determined by machines that extended the mechanical abilities of the body. This was superimposed on the premodern city, which more directly expressed the dimensions of the human body in space. In the postmodern world we are adding layers of electronic technology that imitate our nervous and neurological systems and extend our intellect and communicative abilities. The loss of direct gestural communication as the basic expression of our embodied existence in the city, as it is now increasingly filtered through technology, is both understandable and lamentable. However, there does remain a direct correspondence between the shape of public space and the gestural expressiveness of a culture. For example, this can be determined by comparing the shape of public space in medieval Siena to that of contemporary Los Angeles. The figurally complex public spaces of the medieval city respond to the scale and expressiveness of the slow-moving human body, whereas the spaces of the contemporary city are seemingly indeterminate in structure, understood through accumulated layers of technology.

Our gestural worlds are divided between our private lives and our public personas. The gestural codes we use in private situations with others we know well are very different from those employed in the public realm surrounded by strangers. Both are determined by cultural norms. When these are transgressed we stand out; every culture carefully defines appropriate kinds of public behaviour. The interdependence between a public space and potential public gesticulation depends upon the latent figural structure of the space. The world of action has pre-existing structure and meaning; gestures arise from a prefigured condition.[20] The space for public gesture is, according to Hannah Arendt, a constructed space within which we carry out actions addressed to others, creating a web of human relationships, or narrative order.[21] For the ancient Greeks the *polis* is "the organization of the people as it arises out of acting and speaking together, and its true space lies between people living together for this purpose...."[22] In the contemporary city the vital role of communications between citizens has been displaced into new technologies and spaces.

Alfred Schutz states that we know ourselves through others, by belonging to "a common environment and to be united with the Other in a community of persons...."[23] In other words, to escape from the public realm, as we tend to do, robs us of our human community and self-understanding as mirrored in the actions of others. Beyond the expressiveness and coherence of individual bodily gestures in the public realm, or a shared language, is the need for gestures or bodily events to be assembled into a structure, plot, or narrative. The question remains: Do we accept the condition that Jeff Wall captures in his photographs, with its violent tensions and lack of expression, or do we look to ways in which the expressive potential of public space can be reborn? Or does the contemporary city create new gestural codes?

Gestural codes used in performance, in conjunction with speech, or by the deaf, use combinations of the various types of gestures that Wundt describes: pointing toward, imitating, or symbolizing. Phenomenology implies that gestures, particularly those gestures that are demonstrative and descriptive, can be shared across cultures. Maurice Merleau-Ponty writes:

> The communication or comprehension of gestures comes about through the reciprocity of my intentions and the gestures of others, of my gestures and intentions discernible in the conduct of other people. It is as if the other person's intention inhabited my body and mine his. [24]

Given the chaotic nature of most contemporary spaces, it would seem that what Wundt describes as demonstrative gesture, the most primary form of human gesturing, remains essential as an interpretative and heuristic (i.e., hermeneutical) process that allows the body to constantly find new strategies for anchoring and reorienting itself to the spaces and structures of the city. The city provides the locations to which the body connects itself. The demarcation of boundaries through the gestural extension of the body is a fluid process that builds upon the ephemeral landscapes of the contemporary city. Spaces of the city tend to be open and indeterminate. An ever-changing landscape of structures and surface zoning means that the body is constantly seeking a reorientation; primary forms of gesture unite time and space. The displacement of the expressive and emotive body from the public realm into the private, the realm of intimacy, means the city no longer functions as a gesticulating community. Gestures in public tend to be cryptic, or imply a false sense of intimacy. The spaces of the contemporary city, while lacking expressiveness, still function in developing narrative from the intersections, or events, that the structure engenders. Ultimately, what will emerge are new gestural codes that make sense of contemporary urban environments.

Wundt's second type of gesture, descriptive gesture, is pictorial; the characteristic shapes of things or animals are replicated in a mimetic manner. This form of gesturing populates space with a fleeting metaphoricity; it can transform the mechanistic and informational nature of contemporary space into a world full of anthropomorphic, zoomorphic, and productive qualities. The metaphorical aspects of gesture allow for what Nelson Goodman describes as a "territorial invasion," where one conceptual or poetic schema invades another.[25] This strategy can be critical, a type of guerrilla action, or it can be revelatory, exposing new potentials for the city. The figural aspects of the gestural body can challenge the mechanical and informational structure of urban space.

An extension of the descriptive gesture, symbolic gesture, is another of Wundt's formulations. Here, abstracted codes are employed that have associative power. Symbolic gestures may also have a transcendental power and, like the operations of language, are part of shared understanding. The complex sign languages used by the deaf fall into this category. The gestural languages employed in the city until the nineteenth century, and still maintained in more traditional societies, would also belong here. This is the aspect of the urban gestural space that has largely disappeared, enhanced by the proliferation of electronic technologies. Watching actors on the screen, in the protected comfort of our private worlds, provides a surrogate for our desire to watch the expressive human body. However, as mentioned, there are also examples of thriving urban gestural languages that indicate directions for reinvigorating this aspect of public space.

Can the fecundity of face-to-face communication survive in the contemporary city? There are a number of preliminary ideas that can be drawn from this exploration of gesture. Firstly, there is a close connection between gestural expressiveness and space, and a reciprocity between the constructed world and the body. Secondly, urban designers can learn much from studying theatre and sign language as disciplines that have a highly developed sense of human gesture and spatiality. Thirdly, following Wundt, gestures are demonstrative, descriptive (metaphorical), and symbolic. Fourthly, an investigation into gesture questions the nature and forms of human communication in the city, in the face of ever-proliferating electronic technologies that enhance communication at a distance.

In conclusion, the Polish author Bruno Schulz, writing of Franz Kafka's *The Trial*, describes an important sensitivity regarding gesture when he states:

> Kafka sees the realistic surface of existence with unusual precision, he knows by heart, as it were, its code of gestures, all the external mechanics of events and situations, how they dovetail and interlace, but these to him are but a loose epidermis without roots, which he lifts off like a delicate membrane and fits onto his transcendental world, grafts onto his reality.[26]

Beyond adding an expressive or figural aspect to the spaces of the city, human gestures are gifts to the city, gifts to the strangers who populate any city. Inhibitions, fear, and technological suppression have reduced gesture to a minimum necessary to get by. In order to produce new forms of urban space, designers must understand the fullness of human action. For urban designers a new order of heterogeneous, amorphous, and anomalous spaces must emerge against the banality and predictability of contemporary cities. For example, these spaces could be derived from the spatial figures that arise between two people gesturing toward one another. Conversely, the body does carve out of the indeterminate spaces of the contemporary city spaces that can be comprehended, if only temporarily.

Barcelona, 1994, Graham Livesey

6 POINTS: the PROLIFERATION of INTERSECTIONS

This essay explores "passage," put forward in the introduction, as a word that defines both an urban structure and the corresponding action. Kevin Lynch has written that systems of urban movement and communication "perhaps constitute the most essential functions of a city...."[1] In any city the means of passage most literally describe the functions of the street. The street was the primary space for movement and communication in the traditional or premodern city, and as human technology has evolved, so has the street and its uses. Joseph Rykwert defines the street as "an essential carrier of communication" and "human movement institutionalised."[2] Prior to the Industrial Revolution, the passages or streets of a city were constructed to accommodate pedestrians, animals, and animal-drawn vehicles. Marked out on the ground or defined by dense urban fabric, the premodern street was the principal means of moving goods and knowledge about; it was also the realm for exchange and performance. Traditional streets formed a system of vital public spaces in the city. These qualities of the street emerged from vernacular craft practices where buildings and space were intertwined, and scaled to the human figure. The fabric of the medieval European city with its "organic" structure fulfils this description. By the seventeenth century, the great Baroque streets emerged to accommodate the swift movement of horse-drawn vehicles. Signalling an increased emphasis on the speed of movement, the straight, wide, and perspectivally ordered boulevard indicated that "the man on horseback had taken possession of the city."[3] The linear spaces of the street, within urban structures, remained the principal space of communication until the Industrial Revolution.

In the modern era, waves of mechanical technology transformed the nature and range of human movement and urban form. The train, the automobile, and the aircraft have each shaped urban passage. The advent of the railway and mass transit in the early nineteenth century, in response to new modes of production, greatly enlarged the city horizontally and caused great upheaval in both urban and rural structures. The invention of the elevator by mid-century enabled the city to be extended vertically. Each new mechanical technology opened up new passages in, over, and under the city, parallel corridors of movement and communication that supplemented and transformed the traditional street, adding new layers of complexity to cities.

The modern city emerged from cultures intent on invention, experimentation, and discovery, cultures that produced both the Scientific and Industrial revolutions of the seventeenth and eighteenth centuries. Founded on a progressive drive toward a utopian condition, the primacy of mechanical technologies used to enlarge premodern cities ultimately led to many of the urban models of the nineteenth and twentieth centuries. Lewis Mumford has suggested that the mechanization of the previously organic city, following the Industrial Revolution, was a form of "un-building" where "a more advanced form of life loses its complex character, bringing about an evolution downwards, toward simpler and less finely integrated organisms."[4]

The automobile has probably done more to redefine the traditional public role of the city street than any other technology. The automobile rendered the horse-drawn vehicle obsolete, greatly expanded our horizontal movement (most notably into the countryside and the resulting suburbia), and enhanced our privacy.[5] The overtly private nature of the car and the overblown scale of road and parking systems required to accommodate it severely altered the traditional street that had been carefully scaled to the pedestrian and pre-industrial forms of transportation. In Los Angeles, the glorification of the automobile has generated a wide-open city whose most obvious form of passage is the freeway. The freeway transports goods, people, and information, but is no longer a vital social institution as a place of exchange. The social role provided by older forms of passage has shifted to other urban and suburban locations, notably shopping malls and entertainment complexes.

Since the invention of the telegraph and the discovery of electricity in the nineteenth century, information has been dematerialized; hence, its movement no longer relies on traditional spaces.[6] We have witnessed, during the last few decades, transformations in both urban structure and spatial perception brought on by the rapid growth of "invisible" electronic technologies. This expansion of spatial perception during the modern era has been replaced by an imploded condition, a collapsing of the world reflected in Marshall McLuhan's use of the "village" as a metaphor of the world.[7] Through the use of new forms of communication, global dialogue has been powerfully extended, complemented by worldwide computer networks that create new communities, locally and globally, outside the traditional urban realm. A city such as San José, California, the centre of the computer industry, is an unbounded low-density sprawl traversed by freeways, flight paths, and communications networks connecting elsewhere, in which the traditional street is virtually absent.

Thus, the electronic or post-industrial revolution of the last few decades has radically impacted on the nature of urban space and its use; McLuhan has suggested that electronic technology "bypasses" any previously understood idea of urban space.[8] This has escalated with each new generation of technology, the subsequent implementation of telegraph, radio, telephones, television, and computers. In the contemporary city, the passages are now the airwaves, cables, and fibre optic systems that link together the inhabitants with each other and the world. The netscape, what M. Christine Boyer has described as a "free-floating membrane of connectivity and control,"[9] is an entity where most communication is not restricted to passages that are spatially defined or can be physically moved through. This forms the basis for the virtual city or "cybercity." The information age generates what McLuhan describes as "a total field of inclusive awareness."[10] This notion is reflected in pervasive information technology, the recent phenomenon that layers surfaces, particularly urban surfaces, with ever-changing digital information.

As complex artifacts of human production, responding to cultural needs, cities have transformed from metaphorical representations of the entire human body (the organic city), through the machine city to a structure that is most akin to the nervous system, the informational city, where connectivity is the predominant order.[11] This notion is reflected in McLuhan's statement that whereas "all previous technology (save speech, itself) had, in effect, extended some part of our bodies, electricity may be said to have outered the central nervous system, including the brain."[12] Marshall and Eric McLuhan suggest that the visual preoccupations of scientific and mechanical cultures have given way to a more tactile sense of structures:

> Since electronic man lives in a world of simultaneous information, he finds himself increasingly excluded from his traditional (visual) world, in which space and reason seem to be uniform, connected and stable. Instead, Western (visual and left-hemisphere) man now finds himself habitually relating to information structures that are simultaneous, discontinuous, and dynamic.[13]

In the transfer from the modern to the postmodern the McLuhans argue that we have shifted from a visual definition of space to an acoustic one, from stability to discontinuity, where touch provides the interval of change between structures.

::

Premodern and modern perceptions of urban existence have been transformed by the post-industrial electronic revolution. Traditional structures have given way to more complex and ambiguous systems. The animate organism of the premodern city was transformed into the mechanistic model of the modern city, only to be dramatically restructured into the electronic and informational structure of the contemporary city.

In the premodern city, formally and functionally, streets were distinct from the piazza or square, spaces intended for gathering and lingering. As the primary corridors of movement and communication, streets were integral to the structure of the city. The street intersected either with other streets or with defined public spaces such as the square. Streets linked urban thresholds, such as the gates of the city or the doorways to buildings. Despite the clarity of these junctions, the movement between these systems did not require a dramatic technological or inter-modal transformation; it tended to be a phenomenological, symbolic, or metaphorical transition.

The modern city, transformed by science and industry, saw the emergence of systems of movement that forged new territory both above and below the ground level movement typical of previous cities. Railway, subway, and tramway systems carved their way into the fabric of the older city, dramatically increasing the speed and range of movement and communication in the city. Early "invisible" technologies, such as the telegraph and the telephone, added new layers of communication. In order to interconnect between these systems, the station arose as a necessary urban institution: the railway station, the subway station, and eventually the airport. As Deyan Sudjic has observed, "it is these interchanges from one form of transport to another, and to buildings and public spaces, that are what really create the public life of a city."[14] Lynch has described these essential urban junctions as "nodes," one of a series of elements that make cities comprehensible.[15] In the past century the increased dependency on the airport has replaced both the railway station and the traditional gateway to the city. The airport is now rapidly becoming a destination centre for shopping and entertainment, while continuing to assert its role as a station or transfer point.[16]

McLuhan has called attention to the numerous technologies that shape the contemporary city, noting that "where there are great discrepancies in speeds of movement, as between air and road travel or between telephone and typewriter, serious conflicts occur within organizations."[17] The discrepancies between technologies that McLuhan warns of can constitute a vital new order in the contemporary city. Lynch has described the paths through the city as the most important and comprehensible urban system; however, in cities where there are complex layers of passages, it may be suggested that it is the intersection points, stations, moments of encounter or interface, that are the new urban structure. These points of inter-modal transference provide order in the matrices of systems that make up contemporary cities.

In the contemporary city the mechanistic and linear structures of modern urban passage have given way to a multidirectional network of linear systems that come together as a structure where the intersections are more vital than the passages. These fleeting moments of interface, transformation, or translation between technologies are the postmodern equivalent of the railway or subway station.[18] However, electronic technologies require an instrument in order to render the invisible visible, the inaudible audible, and the illegible legible. The electronic appliance, increasingly portable, is necessary to make the required interface or translation between technologies or media. The gateway and the station have been supplanted by the computer terminal and the cell phone (and other handheld devices), which allow their users to interface immediately with a world of possibilities, to create moments of dialogue anywhere, anytime, anyplace. These points of interface or intersection often have a material and spatial component; they are also the events that enrich the narrative life of contemporary cities.

The transformation of urban passage that began with industrial technology has been accelerated by post-industrial technologies. Contemporary cities are complex superimpositions of technologies. Once the street accommodated all movement and exchange in the city, as information was material and had to be moved physically; the street was scaled to suit the walking or slow-moving individual, who could socially exchange in the same space. Now, many overlaid mechanical and electronic systems perform the same functions with greater speed and complexity. There has been a zoning of the city into parallel systems (subways, railways, freeways, airways, telephone networks, and airwaves) which have tended to exclude the simple urban activities of the pedestrian.

::

There are definitions of the word "passage" that begin to suggest strategies for practice in and inhabitation of the contemporary city. The first is a figural or metaphorical sense of the word that means the "transition from one state or condition to another (*spec.* from this life to the next, by death): the passing or lapse of time; the going on, course or progress of events, etc...."[19] An archaic form of the word suggests that it may also mean something "that 'passes,' goes on, takes place, occurs, or is done; an occurrence, incident or event; an act transaction or proceeding."[20] This is related to "rites of passage," as alluded to in the definition of passage that incorporates moments of transition, and also to narrative structures as suggested by the phrase "progress of events." These moments of transition, or events, extend the linear form of the passage into a comprehensive and multi-layered system that interconnects the systems that comprise any city. Michel Butor affirms the complex nature of sites found in the framework of the city, providing us with a description supporting the notion of the contemporary city as a web, net, matrix, or mosaic.[21] Every site or potential site in a city arises by virtue of its connection to a multiplicity of other sites; this narrative model holds for the postmodern condition. A location comes into being because it is the intersection of differing technologies, of humans and technology, or solely between humans.

If we re-examine the spaces of passage, we can observe that movement has become faster and more wide-ranging, and it has taken on a multiplicity of forms that both complement and destroy traditional aspects of urban structure and existence. Fragmentation, decentralization, and complexity have transformed older forms of order. However, technological evolution, while progressive, is not linear, as we are constantly retrieving aspects of previously lost technologies.[22] This provides for an accumulation of technologies superimposed on each other. Inevitably, existing conditions are altered and new or parallel systems emerge. Despite the vestiges of the traditional street which still thrive in much of the world, its linearity and specificity are obsolete and its functions have been dispersed. What is of relevance to the urban designer are the points of intersection, the stations, nodes, intersections, events, or moments of translation between these various overlaid systems. The loss of urban space scaled to the human figure means that specific locations in space play the vital role in providing the necessary structure (spatial and narrative) for our inhabitation of contemporary cities.

A final relevant definition associated with the word "passage" refers to the "definite passing or travelling from one place to another, by sea, or formerly sometimes by land; a journey; a voyage across the sea from one port to another, a crossing."[23] The reference to crossing suggests a movement with a defined origin and destination or the trajectories of movement that every city comprises; however, the word "journey" extends the meaning of the word into the heuristic realm. The craft and inventive productive paradigms of previous eras have, in postmodern culture, given way to the figure of the *bricoleur*, "someone who plays around with fragments of meaning which he himself has not created."[24] Adrift in a fragmented world, the postmodern figure "wanders about in a labyrinth of commodified light and noise, endeavouring to piece together bits of dispersed narrative."[25] The exploratory nature of current existence is supported by the fragmentary nature of many contemporary urban spaces. The stations and events that mark the intersections between technologies are encountered as part of the daily journeying through the city. Cities cannot be taken for granted, but must continually be challenged as part of an ongoing heuristic process of interpretation.

The physical passages of the city have been rendered less important than the passage of information. The moments of intersection, of translation, or of inter-modal shift create the points, or the moments, in the overlaid networks of the city. Linear structures are arrested by points in space, the proliferation of events that affirm the existence of those who inhabit contemporary cities.

Paris, 1987, Graham Livesey

7 LINES: the CARTOGRAPHIC IDEAL

Lines criss-cross the contemporary city at all levels. They range from those delineated physically, legally, and mentally to the infinite lines of movement that pass through, above, and below the city. As a stroke or mark, and as a basic geometrical element, a line possesses length without breadth. Lines are everywhere: lines of flight, assembly lines, lines of division, power lines, lines of demarcation, transportation lines, lines of text, service lines, property lines, lines of communication, sight lines, and lines of force. Lines can delimit, guide, outline, measure, mark, and imply a course of action (e.g., "line of attack"); lines can unite, but they can also separate, divide, and confine. Lines define the landscape of the city; they produce networks or patterns of overlapping linear systems. Lines also provide the language of operation for various related disciplines: geometry, surveying, navigation, cartography, urban design, and architecture.[1]

Deleuze and Guattari make the distinction between "striated" and "smooth" space in *A Thousand Plateaus: Capitalism and Schizophrenia*:

> … the striated is that which intertwines fixed and variable elements, produces an order and succession

of distinct forms, and organizes horizontal melodic lines and vertical harmonic planes. The smooth is the continuous variation, continuous development of form; it is the fusion of harmony and melody in favor of the properly rhythmic values, the pure act of the drawing of a diagonal across the vertical and horizontal. [2]

These categories provide useful background for discussing the linear dimensions of the contemporary city as both structure and engagement. Striated space refers to the highly ordered structures of sedentary or urban cultures, whereas smooth space is defined by the open spaces of nomadic cultures. The definition and inhabitation of these two kinds of space is fundamentally different; however, as Deleuze and Guattari note, there are situations when these conditions reverse (or overlap) themselves. [3]

The rapid and continuing development of sprawl since the Second World War and the general suburbanization of the city has meant that land that existed as smooth space was striated, first by agricultural activity and then by urbanization. The contemporary city exists in relative flux. This is no more evident than on the periphery, what has been called the *terrain vague*. Here there are no real limits, but an ever-shifting space that creates a kind of frontier, populated by a nesting, but highly mobile, group. And yet there are an abundance of lines within the urban structure of sprawl: subtle, idiosyncratic, shifting, and possibly solipsistic. Linear structures guide the lives of those who live in contemporary urban environments, together with nodal and surface structures.

Lines are used by planners, engineers, and surveyors to set out and manage the city. Lines are used to determine the territoriality of the city, the difference between toxic and non-toxic environments, changing functions (zoning), divisions between classes and races, and how security is managed. The surveyor sets out the limits of the city, of property, of cut and fill, and of buildings. Engineers determine the alignments of systems: lines of movement, lines of supply, lines of force, lines of removal, and power lines. Architects, engineers, and construction companies build structures within the planned, surveyed, and engineered order of the city.

I would like to explore the following types of lines as they apply to the contemporary city: those we cross (networks) or cannot cross (edges), and those we follow (routes) or follow us (trajectories). We cross lines all the time, consciously and unconsciously. Lines that cannot or should not be crossed were more explicit in traditional cities, where the limits of the city were known. In the contemporary city, linear systems shape movement across the city; this tends toward highly controlled movement. Are there opportunities for the meandering, drifting, or diagonal line?

::

While the linear dimensions of the contemporary city are numerous, do any of these provide the existential definition that linear structures provided in traditional cities? Despite the density and complexity of lines in the city, the crossing of most lines goes unnoticed, intersections and thresholds are usually indiscernible, and movement is largely predetermined, customary, and automatic. We follow paths, and communication flows through regulated and modulated channels. Lines link points in space in the striated order of the city; they create the departure and destination points. In nomadic cultures a point in space is secondary, the journey is primary. The endless movement through suburbia, with its paradoxical emphasis on the private realm, diminishes the role of architecture in shaping the public realm, placing emphasis on the journey through space and landscape.[4] Can highly striated cultures that are shifting toward the smooth adapt the smooth space strategies of nomads?

At the point where two lines cross there is an intersection or threshold, a moment or event in time and space. It is the point at which a line of movement crosses a physical line in the city, a border, frontier, or edge. It is passing through an opening. An intersection might be the random crossing of two people (in the street and by telephone), a car accident, the overhead flight of an aircraft, the crossing of two systems or the junction of two streets. An intersection is the transition between modes of technology, the station that defines the transition between pedestrian travel and railway travel. If significant, these intersections or events in space register in some other order; they may weave themselves into a narrative structure. This is only determined if the event contributes to the structure of a plot. Ultimately, the intersection, as a point in space, participates in a larger order of lines, the network. A network is created by a multitude of lines and their crossing points.

In the network of the city there are an infinite number of crossings; it is a highly striated condition. By fluidly changing modes of movement and communication, the linear web can create a landscape that approximates a smooth space. Those moments where an intersection is registered, or in fact prevented, become thresholds or points of resistance. They become events in the ever-unfolding life of the city.

The encounter with the edge, boundary, or frontier defined the spatial and existential limits of the premodern city. The importance of boundaries in traditional cities was particularly poignant in the boundary rituals of classical cultures. The boundary of the city, most clearly delineated by the fortification walls, provided a defensive system, but also a limit to understandable space. The limits of the city and the world were known, the difference between inside and outside, between sacred and profane, and between citizen and foreigner. This clarity was necessary for historic urban cultures. The fixed dimensions of the traditional city are largely gone; other kinds of order have come into play.

In the contemporary city this kind of definition is rare, and usually takes the form of chain-link fencing that has been erected to keep out trespassers. There is no outer edge to the city, as this is a constantly moving condition, and while there may be major divisions within the city between districts and functions, or defined by geographical features (hills, escarpments, rivers, and ravines), these rarely act as profound ordering devices. Lines create division, borders, boundaries, and frontiers. A line creates an edge between two territories. In the contemporary city these are the internal boundaries that separate the rich from the poor. They are the arterial systems that create a closed urban structure defined by inward-looking residential enclaves. As Mike Davis notes, it is the "militarization"[5] of urban space into heavily policed suburban enclaves and gated communities that provides the strongest examples of urban definition.

::

The second set of lines involves those lines we follow or those that leave a trail in our wake. If we are following a route we look ahead for the usual indicators that guide our motion through the city or territory; we follow a line or path. However, when we move in cities, we also leave linear ghosts or traces of our motion. If it is a foray into an unknown territory these lines can be described as trajectories: a target has been determined but the precise line of flight may not be known. According to Kevin Lynch, urban paths provide the predominant orienting system in a city.[6] In suburbia it tends to be the freeway and arterial road systems that provide the governing reference systems. Options for selecting different paths to a destination have been radically reduced by the closed street systems that have replaced the open gridiron structure.[7] Therefore, much movement through a city is predetermined. Routes tend to be homogeneous in their definition, defined more by signage systems than by unique features. As Lynch notes, a route or path should be defined by its distinctiveness, continuity, functionality, directionality, and relationship to topography/landscape.[8] A route is a prescribed movement controlled by the highly striated nature of the city. This can shift to the meandering line of the nomad.

A number of essays on literature by Michel Butor provide insight into the nature of lines, what he usefully calls "trajectories." These link together narrative, the structure of urban space, movement, and writing. According to Butor a city is a sum of trajectories.[9] A trajectory is the passage of something through space and time. It often has a military application such as the "curve described by a projectile in its flight."[10] Butor's use of trajectories is directly linked to notions of narrative, as a sequence of events occurring in space and time.

A trajectory begins somewhere and moves toward some destination; when a line is drawn, it begins and moves toward an ending. A trajectory is a shot in the dark, a journey into an unknown territory, the action of the *flaneur*; it is a heuristic action, a probe or a voyage of discovery. It is the path of life from birth to death. It is also the action of a nomad through a smooth space. Smooth space depends on a radically different form of engagement, where the line of movement defines points or locations in space, rather than the more conventional line between two points.[11] Smooth space requires the actions of a nomad or explorer; orientation constantly changes, is constantly re-evaluated, as one moves through a territory. Nomadic cultures understand and define space differently: smooth space has not been measured, mapped, or subdivided. Reference is not determined by the ordering of the land or the construction of cities. Instead,

> ... the haptic, smooth space of close vision is that its orientations, landmarks, and linkages are in continuous variation; it operates step by step.... Orientations are not constant but change according to temporary vegetation, occupations and precipitation.[12]

110

Michel de Certeau argues that inhabitants of a city are "poets of their own acts, silent discoverers of their own paths in the jungle of functionalist rationality...."[13] Their "wandering lines" are signifying practices, "their trajectories form unforeseeable sentences."[14] The trajectories of movement can subvert the established rules, make the dominant order function in other ways. Intertwined paths of movement give shape to spaces,[15] the "art of composing a path."[16] Urban practices can invent spaces and fictions, edges and routes: these are the strategies of urban living.

The seeming incoherence of the contemporary city is brought into order by the wandering lines of its inhabitants. As de Certeau says, these practices follow popular conventions, but also manage to diverge into new patterns or statements. This language of movement, or choreography, brings harmony to seemingly dissonant structures. These trajectories are essentially figural in that they are narrative and make ephemeral figures in the space of the city and on its surfaces. They can be habitual, aimless, wilful, or directed. They are essential to any inhabitation of an environment. These wanderings are largely unshaped by urban form, but they give the contemporary city its legitimacy.

::

The homogeneity of sprawl has meant that a highly structured or striated environment has become like the smooth space of nomadic cultures. Therefore, we discover that nomadic strategies of movement can give order to the indeterminate structure of sprawl. This is consistent with the idea that a general or universal space, the space of modernity, dominates the contemporary city. In smooth space the line of the journey is a "vector, a direction and not a dimension or metric determination."[17] Space is created by local operations and filled with events.[18]

The lines of movement, or lines of force, through a territory continually define or redefine that territory.[19] Every line that constitutes a part of a city, whether engaged or not, determines, even fleetingly, a territory. For example, the relentless movement of vehicles across and through the city, is a kind of scribbling action, incessant and trivial, a back and forth that leaves no discernible condition. It may only be the territory of that line, the link between A and B. However, more likely it is part of some circumscription.

This networking together of a city or territory through both the construction of the landscape and the actions of inhabitants gives any city its vitality. The contemporary city's emphasis on space and shifting definitions means that these actions are necessarily heuristic (a searching) and hermeneutic (interpretative). Every site in a city is connected to every other site. An infinitely complex web establishes the potential in an urban structure. Many lines will never be travelled or activated; they are standing potential. Within the striated order of the city is always present the smooth space of nomads; there is a passage from striated to smooth, and from smooth to striated.

The city can be understood as an infinite complexity of lines, made up of networks and edges, routes and trajectories. According to Deleuze:

> One might say in a certain sense that what is primary in a society are the lines, the movements of flight. For, far from being a flight from the societal, far from being utopian or even ideological, these constitute the social field, trace out its gradation and its boundaries, the whole of its becoming. [20]

These lines control and pattern space. Ultimately lines determine the degree to which a city is structurally open or closed, is easy or difficult to transgress. The navigational dimensions of urban lines provide the intrepid citizen with a multitude of strategies and narrative linkages. A "line of drift" intersects a "customary line"; these lines compose a map, a cartography of actions. [21] It is the diagonal movement across the landscape that challenges the striated order of the contemporary city.

Montreal, 1987, Graham Livesey

8 SURFACES: the ROLE of MEMORY

> The past is everywhere. All around us lie features
> which, like ourselves and our thoughts, have more
> or less recognizable antecedents. Relics, histories,
> memories suffuse human experience. Each par-
> ticular trace of the past ultimately perishes, but
> collectively they are immortal. Whether it is cel-
> ebrated or rejected, attended or ignored, the past is
> omnipresent.[1]

Many of the contemporary cities of the world seem to be
places of forgetting. They appear shallow and ephemeral,
ever-changing landscapes of unrelated elements, zoned
by patterns of communication and constructed of materials unreceptive to memory. North American cities, in
particular, where buildings come and go with alarming
rapidity and the private realm is emphasized, tend not
to value buildings for their ability to maintain collective
memory. This essay searches for the locations of memory
in the structure of the contemporary city.

What is memory? Memory is that by which things
are remembered, a faculty of the human body, the capac-
ity to revive the past. Memory is the act of remembering

or recollection, bringing the past into the present, often as a way of informing the future. A memory is something we hold regarding a thing, person or event that occurred in the past. It is the time during which a recollection endures. It is the act of commemoration, the recording or preserving of the past through ritual action, writing (history) or making. Memory also encompasses the numerous technologies and devices we make to house the past: books, computers, memorials, souvenirs, monuments, and the like. Memories belong both to the individual and to the collective.[2]

Memory encompasses action: we live memory through our embodiment and social needs. Memory arises in encounters with others in the world, from the events that comprise any life. The world would be meaningless if we had no memory, either recollected, dreamed, or habitually enacted through our bodies. Memories are intimately bound to place; this attachment provides identity and orientation. We share a history with landscapes in order to recognize them; previous encounters make things in the present comprehensible. The past renders the present familiar, enabling us to recognize ourselves in our environments. Memory is vital to recognition, to understanding the world through a certain familiarity. For those who are dislocated, or thrust into unfamiliar worlds, this rupture can lead to a loss of identity, akin to a loss of memory.

A city, as a collection of strangers, is dependent on its shared memory in order to remain coherent. Memories emerge from the actions of urban dwellers, from events, both large and trivial, that occur: a great public sporting event, the funeral of a luminary, or a collision with someone on a street. The life of a city is strongly held in the stories the citizens evolve from their actions. Paradoxically, memories can become more enduring as the material of the city slowly disappears. Cities are humankind's greatest material expression of collective memory.

Maurice Halbwachs, in his seminal study *The Collective Memory*, maintains that there is an intimate reciprocity between a group or collective and the space it inhabits: one imprints upon the other.[3] Most groups "engrave their form in some way upon the soil and retrieve their collective remembrances within the spatial framework thus defined."[4] This engraving of past events into the structure of the city is captured in the following quotation from Italo Calvino:

> The city [Zaira], however, does not tell its past, but contains it like the lines of a hand, written in the corners of the streets, the gratings of the windows, the banisters of the steps, the antennae of the lightning rods, the poles of the flags, every segment marked in turn with scratches, indentations, scrolls.[5]

The marks left over time by the inhabitants of a city on its surfaces provide the traces of memory. As Calvino suggests, a city should be a container, or vessel, for memories.

In an examination of memory, E.W. Straus provides a useful model with his concept of the "memory trace."[6] Straus defines a memory trace as "the residue, the deposit of a past event in a receiving material"[7] and that "in a trace, the past is preserved in the present as past."[8] A memory trace "contains less but also more than the original event."[9] Straus cogently argues that memory traces are imprints left in a material by an event in the past. A trace preserves only a fragment of a past event; it is inherently fragile. The receiving material must have a certain plasticity, to be welcome to the actions upon it. He notes that the "receiving material must compensate for the transitoriness of the event."[10] At the formation of the trace the event and the material act together. A trace is an inadvertent act of creation; a transformation occurs that produces an artifact that can be interpreted.

According to Straus traces must be interpreted as artifacts, as each, if properly read, can reveal a story. The ability to reconstruct a past event requires careful interpretation, as examining fragmentary evidence in order to reconstruct a memory demands a practised eye. The city can be read in the sense of a detective searching for the clues of a crime: the detritus and scars of the past reveal much to those open to their interpretation. Reading unlocks a story in an artifact, a "historical reconstruction." Traces bring the past into the present. Grasping and reconstructing the past through the reading of traces is an act of hermeneutics. [11]

Artifacts appeal directly and concretely to our senses. According to David Lowenthal, the past "surrounds and saturates us; every scene, every statement, every action retains residual content from earlier times." [12] He goes on to write that the "facets of the past that live on in our gestures and words, rules and artifacts, appear to us as 'past' only when we know them as such." [13] Relics, artifacts of our past, are worn away by time, and earlier structures give way to subsequent ones. [14] Relics belong to the past and the present simultaneously. No artifact is static; they age, they are altered, and they become, in some cases, obsolete. Artifacts of memory are past and present, historical and modern, they "enlarge today's landscapes." [15]

A city is an ideal recording device, an endless landscape of artifacts open to the actions of time. For example, the British writer Iain Sinclair reads the traces of London's past in his book, *Lights Out For The Territory.* Describing his objective in the opening paragraph, he writes:

> The notion was to cut a crude V into the sprawl of the city ... recording and retrieving the messages on walls, lampposts, doorjambs: the spites and spasms

> of a deranged populace ... a subterranean, precon-
> scious text capable of divination and prophecy.[16]

Rainer Maria Rilke reads traces of the past on the divid-
ing walls between houses exposed by demolition:

> ... the most unforgettable things were the walls
> themselves. The stubborn life of these rooms had not
> let itself be trampled out. It was still there; it clung to
> the nails that were left, stood on the narrow remnant
> of flooring, crouched under the corner beams where
> a bit of interior still remained.... There the noons
> lingered, and the illnesses, and the exhalations, and
> the smoke of many years.... [17]

The contemporary Catalan artist Antoni Tàpies has also
explored the walls of the city in numerous paintings.
Describing his discoveries, he writes:

> The image of the wall can contain countless sug-
> gestions. Separation, claustrophobia, wailing walls,
> prison walls, rejection of the world, contemplation,
> destruction of passion, silence, death, laceration,
> torture, torn bodies, human debris.... [18]

Tàpies reveals the materiality of walls in thick paintings
that use impasto as a medium. He mimics the actions of

weather, time, and graffiti artists to produce works dense with memory traces.

Every new trace alters the order of the city in some elusive way, enriching the ever-evolving story of the city.[19] An artifact or landscape is transformed, often subtly, by the passage of time. The ephemeral actions of the inhabitants are etched onto the walls, ground, and paraphernalia that make up the material of the city. The evolution of a city, through development, demolition, and disaster, provides material to be deciphered. This reminds us that the constructed city is susceptible to the ravages of time, and like the body, it ages and, given enough time, can virtually disappear. The infinite marks, stains, lines, and erosions left on a city describe a text, a text that appears on every surface. Of course, many events leave no trace whatsoever, as decipherable traces constitute only a portion of the history of the city.

Traditionally, the walls and surfaces of a city provided a suitable material for receiving the actions of its inhabitants and the elements over time. The ongoing inhabitation and construction of a city relies to a large extent on memory. The spaces of a city frame the actions that become memory, that are the actions of someone or a group remembering. Beyond the random and inadvertent traces we make, and because we are constantly threatened by forgetting, we surround ourselves with a plethora of reminders, devices that support our memories, and hence our existence.[20] The objects of our memory are the numerous artifacts we employ to house our memory, both consciously and unconsciously. Often they are used to aid us in recalling something we wish to remember, reminders that our memories are fallible, that we are liable to forgetting. Locations in the spaces of a city act as both collective and personal mnemonic devices, elements that trigger a memory.

Pierre Nora argues that there has been a decline in collective memory. Where once memory was generally part of environments, it has been reduced to limited and specific locations.[21] The sites of memory, for Nora, are defined by the material, the symbolic, and the functional which are all present. These sites are created by a "play" of memory, or a "will to remember."[22] The most basic purpose of these sites is to "stop time, to block the work of forgetting, to establish a state of things, to immortalize death, to materialize the immaterial."[23] They exist because of their ability to metamorphose. The sites of memory, which are not always obvious, can be mapped and range from the monumental to the insignificant.

Nora states that memory has now become largely an archival activity, dependent on preserving the material traces from the past.[24] Memory's "new vocation is to record; delegating to the archive the responsibility of remembering."[25] The decline of memory as a vital aspect of cultures is also reflected in the loss of ritual. Centuries ago the emergence of writing displaced memory from the active traditions of oral cultures to the relative precision and endurance of the past in text.[26] Memory, as a living force, has been replaced by history as a way of preserving the past. Nora notes that memory "takes root in the concrete, in spaces, gestures, images and objects."[27] He suggests that now memory resides only in empty gestures; the immediate and spontaneous action of a culture, sustained by memory, has been lost.

Does the contemporary city function as a mnemonic device?

The imprints of past events on the receiving material of the city are abundant in older cities where stone and brick have worn for long periods of time. Imprinting memory into a receiving material allows for some level of posterity to occur. However, the materiality of the traditional city has been supplanted by an emphasis on space and movement, rendering the form of the city less important.[28] The contemporary city does not lend itself to similar actions. The current materials of construction are either too hard, too pristine, or too mediocre to act as a suitable receiving medium for the actions of the past.[29] In the contemporary city of glass that is constantly cleaned, of inferior materials that deteriorate and are quickly replaced, and with an emphasis on space that often negates building, this is particularly so. It is in the neglected and forlorn parts of cities that memory traces endure the longest, where there is not the ability to erase them with new development. Generally, there is a lack of "plasticity" in the architecture of the contemporary city.

A city's surfaces are only one receiving material for the traces of memory. The technologies of writing, photography, film, and recording are others. The proliferation of communications technologies has displaced, eroded, and historicized memory. The advent of computer technology means that the architecture of the city receives less of cultural memory than it once did. Memory remains an elusive aspect of the body/mind/world continuum. As Elaine Scarry notes:

> … certain complex characteristics of the embodied human being have no (or as yet, no known) physical location or mechanism. The printing press, the institutionalized convention of written history, photographs, libraries, films, tape recordings, and Xerox machines are all materializations of the elusive embodied capacity for *memory*.… They together make a relatively ahistorical creature into a historical one, one whose memory extends far back beyond the opening of its own individual experience.… [30]

This elusiveness is manifest in the electronic revolution of the past several decades. A dynamic and living collective memory has been supplanted by the static and obsessive archival work of historians. Cities have become great archives or data banks of memory for the manufacture of history, supported by institutions, governments, and economies. Various works of architecture deal explicitly with memory, in that they house its manifestations: monuments, cemeteries, museums, cinemas, and libraries. Every fragment from the past, both distant and recent, is housed. This coincides with Pierre Nora's argument that contemporary societies are more concerned with archiving material for historical purposes than maintaining a living collective memory. The collective memory has been fragmented into a plethora of memories and histories, representing in effect the privatization of memory.

As an artifact, the contemporary city more clearly extends the brain and nervous system than it does other aspects of the human body. Populated by electronic technologies able to reproduce or store enormous amounts of information, the city has been redefined as a mnemonic device. This is reflected in the surfaces of glass and steel that shelter the silently accumulating memory banks of contemporary culture.

::

The most stable level of the city seems to be the ground plane, which is typically ignored. Covered in elusive and endless structures, trenched by infrastructure, the ground upon which a city lies records across time all the excavations, constructions, and disasters, both human and natural. Vestiges of structures that are ruined or demolished, the endless cycle of building, decay, transformation, and destruction leaves its evidence for those who can decipher the remains. A city remembers many dimensions on the ground: legal, religious, and social. Halbwachs shows that the laws pertaining to the ownership and control of land are reflected in the organization of streets, shape of lots, zoning, and building types. The nature of religion determines the distinctions between sacred and profane space, evident, for instance, in the design and location of temples and cemeteries. Social structure organizes the city according to class, activity, wealth, and religion.[31] The ground has a resilience and ability to record not provided by any other aspect of the city. Placing an emphasis on the ground on which a city is built evokes Heidegger's notion of the earth as "serving bearer."[32] The ground is to be preserved as it supports the city and stores the past, waiting for the careful attentions of the archaeologist.

The housing of memory in the contemporary city has changed when compared with previous periods in the history of the city. The displacement of urban memory is particularly evident if one uses Straus's notion of the memory trace. Much of this has to do with the technological exploits of the twentieth century. Architecture receptive to memory, as a spontaneous aspect of human culture, has been displaced by modernity, the manufacture of history, and electronic technologies. The spaces of the city, private and public, once the settings within which our memories were made and stored, like the body itself, have become unreadable.

The world provides points of attachment to which we anchor our memories and ourselves. A city should be understood as constructed memory. The material aspect of the city (the buildings, infrastructure, and landscapes) provides a record of a city's past desires. At any given moment in time every city comprises a constructed record of its history, a collective memory. During our lives our memories are intimately related to space; in fact they make space intimate, through a reciprocity. We associate events in our past with the places in which they occurred. When we revisit those locations our past and present are remarkably fused. We have marked the city with our memories; it provides us with landmarks and provides orientation. When we visit a new city, previous cities we have inhabited or visited crowd our experience.

A city can be described as an assemblage of many of the things we make as humans, as extensions of the body. It is a constructed field of action, defined by a complex wealth of boundaries, paths, systems, spaces, and artifacts. A city should support memory in its many and diverse guises. To be aware of the operations of memory in an urban context can help architects, planners, politicians, and citizens maintain environments, not just as static or nostalgic creations. Memory truly comes alive when it is acted upon. Through imagination we are led to invention; our cultural memory guides our actions in an informed way. Our past lives in the actions of the present; our actions and artifacts are, to a large extent, informed by our past.

129

London, 1987, Graham Livesey

SELECT BIBLIOGRAPHY

Butor, Michel. *Inventory: Essays by Michel Butor.* Ed. Richard Howard. New York: Simon and Schuster, 1968.

Calvino, Italo. *Invisible Cities.* Trans. William Weaver. New York: Harvest/HJB, 1974.

de Certeau, Michel. *The Practice of Everyday Life.* Trans. Steven Rendall. Berkeley: University of California Press, 1984.

de Duve, Thierry, Arielle Pelenc, and Boris Groys. *Jeff Wall.* London: Phaidon, 1995.

Deleuze, Gilles, and Felix Guattari. *A Thousand Plateaus: Capitalism and Schizophrenia.* Trans. Brian Massumi. Minneapolis: University of Minnesota Press, 1987.

Hill, Edward. *The Language of Drawing.* Englewood Cliffs: Prentice-Hall, 1966.

Halbwachs, Maurice. *The Collective Memory.* Trans. Francis J. Ditter, Jr. and Vida Yazdi Ditter. New York: Harper & Row, 1980.

Kearney, Richard. *The Wake of Imagination.* Minneapolis: University of Minnesota Press, 1988.

Kerby, Anthony Paul. *Narrative and the Self.* Bloomington: Indiana University Press, 1991.

Lefebvre, Henri. *The Production of Space.* Trans. Donald Nicholson-Smith. Oxford: Blackwell, 1991.

Lynch, Kevin. *The Image of the City.* Cambridge, Mass.: MIT Press, 1960.

McLuhan, Marshall. *Understanding Media.* New York: McGraw-Hill, 1964.

Pope, Albert. *Ladders.* New York: Princeton Architectural Press, 1996.

Ricoeur, Paul. *The Rule of Metaphor*. Trans. Robert Czerny, with Kathleen McLaughin and John Costello. Toronto: University of Toronto Press, 1977.

———. *Time and Narrative*. Vol. 1. Trans. Kathleen McLaughlin and David Pellauer. Chicago: University of Chicago Press, 1984.

Rykwert, Joseph. *The Necessity of Artifice*. New York: Rizzoli, 1982.

Sacks, Oliver. *Seeing Voices: A Journey into the World of the Deaf.* Berkeley and Los Angeles: University of California Press, 1989.

Sacks, Sheldon (ed.). *On Metaphor*. Chicago: University of Chicago Press, 1978.

Scarry, Elaine. *The Body in Pain: The Making and Unmaking of the World*. New York: Oxford University Press, 1985.

Schulz, Bruno, *The Complete Fiction of Bruno Schulz*. Trans. Celina Wieniewska. New York: Walker & Co., 1989.

Sennett, Richard. *The Fall of Public Man*. New York: Vintage Books, 1978.

Sorkin, Michael (ed.). *Variations on a Theme Park: the New American City and the End of Public Space*. New York: Noonday Press, 1992.

Venturi, Robert, *Complexity and Contradiction in Architecture*. New York: The Museum of Modern Art, 1977.

Venturi, Robert, Denise Scott Brown, and Steven Izenour. *Learning from Las Vegas*. Cambridge, Mass.: MIT Press, 1972.

Wundt, Wilhelm. *The Language of Gestures*. Trans. J.S. Thoyer, C.M. Greeleaf, and M.D. Silberman. The Hague: Mouton, 1973.

NOTES

introduction

1   Jonathan Raban, *Soft City* (Glasgow: Fontana/Collins, 1975), 10.

2   "Passage," *Oxford English Dictionary*, 2nd ed., vol. 11 (Oxford: Clarendon Press, 1989), 301.

3   Ibid., 300.

4   See Richard Kearney, *The Wake of Imagination* (Minneapolis: University of Minnesota Press, 1988), 12–13.

essay one

1   Henri Lefebvre, *The Production of Space*, Donald Nicholson-Smith, trans. (Oxford: Blackwell, 1991), 8.

2   Michel Foucault, "Of Other Spaces: Utopias and Heterotopias," in Neil Leach, ed., *Rethinking Architecture: A Reader in Cultural Theory* (London: Routledge, 1997), 350.

3   See, for example, Peter Collins, *Changing Ideals in Modern Architecture 1750–1950* (Montreal: McGill-Queen's University Press, 1967); Cornelis van de Ven, *Space in Architecture: the Evolution of a New Idea in the Theory and History of the Modern Movements* (Amsterdam: Van Gorcum Assen, 1978); and Reyner Banham, *Age of the Masters* (London: The Architectural Press, 1975).

4   Banham, *Age of the Masters*, 51.

5   See Henry-Russell Hitchcock and Philip Johnson, *The International Style* (New York: W.W. Norton, 1966).

6   For instance, the Dutch De Stijl movement, Russian Constructivism, the Bauhaus, the several architectural offshoots of Cubism, and the various *Neue Sachlichkeit* groups in Germany, Switzerland, and Holland.

135

7   Robert Venturi, Denise Scott Brown, and Steven Izenour, *Learning From Las Vegas* (Cambridge, MA: MIT Press, 1972), 81.

8   Albert Pope, *Ladders* (New York: Princeton Architectural Press, 1996), 3–5.

9   Ibid., 61.

10   Susan Sontag, *Under the Sign of Saturn* (New York: Farrar, Straus & Giroux, 1980), 117.

11   Lefebvre, *The Production of Space*, 313.

12   Frederic Jameson, "Postmodernism or the Cultural Logic of Late Capitalism," *New Left Review* 145 (1984): 84.

13   Lefebvre, *The Production of Space*, 83.

14   Ibid., 73.

15   Ibid., 170.

16   Ibid., 57.

17   Michel de Certeau, *The Practice of Everyday Life*, Steven Rendall, trans. (Berkeley: University of California Press, 1984), 117.

18   Ibid.

19   Lefebvre, *The Production of Space*, 164.

20   Foucault, "Of Other Spaces," 354.

essay two

1   Robert Venturi, *Complexity and Contradiction in Architecture* (New York: Museum of Modern Art, 1977), 41.

2   "Anomaly," *Funk & Wagnalls Standard Dictionary* (New York: Harper & Row, 1983), 27.

3   Venturi, *Complexity and Contradiction*, 41.

4   Ibid.

5   John Summerson, *Heavenly Mansions, and other Essays on Architecture* (New York: W.W. Norton, 1963), 189–90.

6   Jonathan Culler, *On Deconstruction: Theory and Criticism after Structuralism* (Ithaca: Cornell University Press, 1983), 97.

7   Jonathan Culler, cited in Michael Benedikt, *Deconstructing the Kimbell: An Essay on Meaning and Architecture* (New York: Sites Books, 1991), 10.

8   Lefebvre, *The Production of Space*, 373, 395–97.

9   Ibid., 395.

10 Ibid., 373.

11 Culler, *On Deconstruction*, 110.

essay three

1   Paul Ricoeur, "Life; A Story in Search of a Narrator," in M.C. Doeser and J.N. Kraay, eds., *Facts and Values: Philosophical Reflections from Western and Non-Western Perspectives* (Dordrecht: Martinus Nijhoff, 1986), 121.

2   Paul Ricoeur, *Time and Narrative*, vol. 1, Kathleen McLaughlin and David Pellauer, trans. (Chicago: University of Chicago Press, 1984), xi.

3   Paul Ricoeur, *The Rule of Metaphor*, Robert Czerny, with Kathleen McLaughlin and John Costell, trans. (Toronto: University of Toronto Press, 1977), 6.

4   Ricoeur, *Time and Narrative*, vol. 1, 41.

5   Ibid., 54.

6   Ibid., 64.

7   Ibid., 65.

8   Ibid., 71.

9   Anthony Paul Kerby, *Narrative and the Self* (Bloomington: Indiana University Press, 1991), 43.

10 Nigel Coates, "Narrative Break-up," in *Themes 3: The Discourse of Events* (London: Architectural Association, 1983), 17.

11 Michel Butor, *Inventory: Essays by Michel Butor*, Richard Howard, ed. (New York: Simon and Schuster, 1968), 27.

12 Ibid. 22.

13   de Certeau, *The Practice of Everyday Life*, 35.

14   Butor, *Inventory*, 19.

15   Ibid., 37.

16   Ibid., 22.

17   Peter G. Rowe, *Design Thinking* (Cambridge, MA: MIT Press, 1987), 34.

18   Ricoeur, "Life; A Story in Search of a Narrator," 127.

19   De Certeau, *The Practice of Everyday Life*, xviii.

20   Ibid., 34.

21   Ibid., 97.

22   Ibid., 97–98.

23   Ibid., 99.

24   Kerby, *Narrative and the Self,* 52.

essay four

1   Michel Leiris, *Brisées: Broken Branches*, Lydia Davis, trans. (San Francisco: North Point Press, 1989), 18.

2   Terence Hawkes, *Metaphor* (London: Methuen, 1972), 1.

3   George Lakoff and Mark Johnson, *Metaphors We Live By* (Chicago: University of Chicago Press, 1980), 5.

4   Hawkes, *Metaphor*, 1.

5   Ibid., 2.

6   Ernst Cassirer, *Language and Myth*, Suzanne K. Langer, trans. (New York: Dover, 1953), 95.

7   Philip Wheelwright, *Metaphor and Reality* (Bloomington: Indiana University Press, 1962), 92.

8   Paul Ricoeur, "Word, Polysemy, Metaphor: Creativity in Language," in Mario J. Valdés, ed., *A Ricoeur Reader: Reflection & Imagination* (Toronto: University of Toronto Press, 1991), 65.

9   Ibid., 70.

10   Ibid., 85.

11   Nelson Goodman, *Languages of Art* (Indianapolis: Bobbs-Merrill, 1968), 73.

12   James M. Edie, *Speaking and Meaning: The Phenomenology of Language Reality* (Bloomington: Indiana University Press, 1976), 188.

13   See Christine Brooke-Rose, *A Grammar of Metaphor* (London: Secker & Warburg, 1958). See also the work of Lakoff and Johnson.

14   Ibid., 17.

15   See, for example, Donald Davidson, "What Metaphors Mean," in Shelson Sacks, ed., *On Metaphor* (Chicago: University of Chicago Press, 1978).

16   David E. Cooper, *Metaphor* (Oxford: Blackwell, 1986), 19.

17   See Jacques Derrida, "White Mythology: Metaphor in the Text of Philosophy," in *Margins of Philosophy* (New York: Harvester Wheatsheaf, 1982).

18   Ricoeur, *The Rule of Metaphor,* 285.

19   Ricoeur, *Time and Narrative,* vol. 1, xi.

20   Paul Ricoeur, "The Metaphorical Process as Cognition, Imagination, and Feeling," in Sheldon Sacks, ed., *On Metaphor* (Chicago: University of Chicago Press, 1978), 141.

21   Ibid., 142.

22   Ibid., 143.

23   Ibid.. 144.

24   Ibid., 145.

25   Ibid.

26   Ibid.

27   Ibid., 149.

28   Ibid., 151.

29   Ibid., 154.

30   Ricoeur, "Word, Polysemy, Metaphor," 79.

31 Anselm L. Straus, *Images of the American City* (New York: The Free Press, 1961), 8.

32 Ibid., 14.

33 This is particularly evident in the work of Francesco di Giorgio. See Anthony Vidler, "The Building in Pain: The Body and Architecture in Post-Modern Culture," *AA Files 19* (Spring 1990), 4.

34 Joseph Rykwert, ed., *Ten Books on Architecture by L.B. Alberti* (London: Alec Tiranti, 1965), 83.

35 Ibid., 100.

36 Le Corbusier, *The City of Tomorrow and its Planning*, Frederick Etchells, trans. (London: The Architectural Press, 1971), 1.

37 Ibid., 131.

38 Deyan Sudjic, *100 Mile City* (London: André Deutsch, 1992), 308.

39 Ibid., 143.

40 See Michael H. Cowan, *City of the West: Emerson, America and Urban Metaphor* (New Haven: Yale University Press, 1967).

41 Straus, *Images of the American City*, 108.

42 Ibid., 175–76.

43 Ibid., 126.

44 Ibid., 177.

45 Ibid., 18–32.

46 Ibid., 41.

47 Ibid., 42.

48 See Elaine Scarry, *The Body in Pain: The Making and Unmaking of the World* (New York: Oxford University Press, 1985).

49 See Vidler, "The Building in Pain."

50 Aldo van Eyck, quoted in A. Smithson, ed., *Team 10 Primer* (Cambridge, MA: MIT Press, 1968), 129.

51   Burton Pike, *The Image of the City in Modern Literature* (Princeton: Princeton University Press, 1981), 129.

52   Edie, *Speaking and Meaning*, 193–94.

53   Pike, *The Image of the City*, 129.

essay five

1   See Richard Sennett, *The Fall of Public Man* (New York: Vintage Books, 1978).

2   Ibid., 39.

3   Jeff Wall, "Gestus," in Thierry de Duve, Arielle Pelenc, and Boris Groys, *Jeff Wall* (London: Phaidon Press, 1996), 76.

4   Ibid.

5   Sennett, *The Fall of Public Man*, 29.

6   Mary Margaret Robb and Lester Thonssen, eds. (Carbondale: Southern Illinois University Press, 1966).

7   See Elijah Anderson, "Street Etiquette and Street Wisdom," in Philip Kasinitz, ed., *Metropolis: Center and Symbol of Our Times* (New York: NYU Press, 1995).

8   Oliver Sacks, *Seeing Voices: A Journey into the World of the Deaf* (Berkeley and Los Angeles: University of California Press, 1989), 87.

9   Ibid., 89.

10   Ibid., 76. The concept of the "grammaticization of space" Sacks attributes to Edward S. Klima and Ursula Bellugi.

11   Chicago : University of Chicago Press, 1992.

12   Wilhelm Wundt, *The Language of Gestures,* J.S. Thayer, C.M. Greenleaf, and M.D. Silberman, trans. (The Hague: Mouton, 1973), 74.

13   Ibid., 76.

14   Ibid.

15   Ibid.

16   Ibid., 78–81.

17   Ibid., 84.

18   Ibid., 84–87.

19   See Scarry, *The Body in Pain*.

20   See Ricoeur, *Time and Narrative,* vol. 1, 54.

21   See Hannah Arendt, *The Human Condition* (Chicago: University of Chicago Press, 1958), 175–247.

22   Ibid., 198.

23   Alfred Schutz, *On Phenomenology and Social Relations*, Helmut R. Wagner, ed. (Chicago: University of Chicago Press, 1970), 164.

24   Maurice Merleau-Ponty, *Phenomenology of Perception*, Colin Smith, trans. (London: Routledge & Kegan Paul, 1962), 185.

25   See Goodman, *Languages of Art*.

26   Jerzy Ficowski, ed., *Letters and Drawings of Bruno Schulz*, Walter Arndt and Victoria Nelson, trans. (New York: Fromm, 1990), 88.

essay six

1   Kevin Lynch, "The Pattern of the Metropolis," in L. Rodwin, ed., *The Future Metropolis* (New York: George Brazilier, 1961), 104.

2   Joseph Rykwert, *The Necessity of Artifice* (New York: Rizzoli, 1982), 105.

3   Lewis Mumford, *The City in History* (New York: Harcourt, Brace & World, 1961), 371.

4   Ibid., 451.

5   See Marshall McLuhan, *Understanding Media* (New York: McGraw-Hill, 1964), 217–25.

6   Ibid., 89.

7   Ibid., 225.

8   Ibid., 104–5.

9   M. Christine Boyer, "The Imaginary Real World of Cybercities," *Assemblage 18* (1992), 117.

10   McLuhan, *Understanding Media*, 104.

11   See Boyer, "The Imaginary Real World of Cybercities."

12   McLuhan, *Understanding Media*, 247.

13   Marshall and Eric McLuhan, *Laws of Media: The New
      Science* (Toronto: University of Toronto Press, 1988),
      102.

14   Deyan Sudjic, *The 100 Mile City* (London: Flamingo,
      1992), 285.

15   See Kevin Lynch, *The Image of the City* (Cambridge,
      MA: MIT Press, 1960).

16   See Paul Virilio, "The Overexposed City," in *The Lost
      Dimension*, Daniel Moshenberg, trans. (New York:
      Semiotext(e), 1991).

17   McLuhan, *Understanding Media*, 91.

18   Sudjic, *The 100 Mile City*, 285.

19   "Passage," *Oxford English Dictionary*, 2nd ed., vol. 11
      (Oxford: Clarendon Press, 1989), 300.

20   Ibid., 301.

21   Butor, *Inventory*, 37.

22   Marshall and Eric McLuhan, *Laws of Media*, 102.

23   "Passage," *Oxford English Dictionary*, 2nd ed., vol. 11,
      301.

24   Kearney, *The Wake of Imagination*, 13.

25   Ibid.

essay seven

  1   "Line," *Oxford English Dictionary*, 2nd ed., vol. 8
       (Oxford: Clarendon Press, 1989), 973–79.

  2   Gilles Deleuze and Felix Guattari, *A Thousand Plateaus:
       Capitalism and Schizophrenia*, Brian Massumi, trans.
       (Minneapolis: University of Minnesota Press, 1987),
       478.

  3   Ibid., 474.

  4   Ibid., 478.

5   See Mike Davis, "Fortress Los Angeles: The Militarization of Urban Space," in Michael Sorkin, ed., *Variations on a Theme Park* (New York: Noonday Press, 1992).

6   Lynch, *The Image of the City*, 49.

7   See Albert Pope, *Ladders*.

8   Lynch, *The Image of the City*, 49–62.

9   Butor, *Inventory*, 36.

10   "Trajectory," *Oxford English Dictionary*, 2nd ed., vol. 18 (Oxford: Clarendon Press, 1989), 376.

11   Deleuze and Guattari, *A Thousand Plateaus*, 488.

12   Ibid., 493.

13   De Certeau, *The Practice of Everyday Life*, xviii.

14   Ibid.

15   Ibid., 97.

16   Ibid., 100.

17   Deleuze and Guattari, *A Thousand Plateaus*, 478.

18   Ibid., 493.

19   Ibid., 55.

20   Constantin V. Boundas, ed., *The Deleuze Reader* (New York: Columbia University Press, 1993), 233.

21   Deleuze and Guattari, *A Thousand Plateaus*, 203.

essay eight

1   David Lowenthal, *The Past is a Foreign Country* (Cambridge: Cambridge University Press, 1985), xv.

2   "Memory," *Oxford English Dictionary*, 2nd ed., vol. 9 (Oxford: Clarendon Press, 1989), 596–98.

3   Maurice Halbwachs, *The Collective Memory*, Francis J. Ditter, Jr. and Vida Yazdi Ditter, trans. (New York: Harper & Row, 1980), 130.

4   Ibid., 156.

5   Italo Calvino, *Invisible Cities*, William Weaver, trans. (New York: Harvest/HBJ, 1974), 11.

6 "Trace," *Oxford English Dictionary,* 2nd ed., vol. 18 (Oxford: Clarendon Press, 1989), 332–33. According to the dictionary the word "trace" as a noun means: the "track made by the passage of any person or thing"; "vestiges or marks remaining indicating the former presence, existence, or action of something"; "a line or figure drawn"; and "the track described by a moving point, line or surface." As a verb it means: "to discover, find out, or ascertain by investigation"; to "make marks upon"; "to draw an outline or figure of."

7 Erwin W. Straus, *Phenomenological Psychology: the Selected Papers of Erwin W. Straus,* Erling Eng, trans. (London: Tavistock Publications, 1966), 85.

8 Ibid., 90.

9 Ibid., 86.

10 Ibid., 85.

11 Paul Ricoeur meditates on the notion of traces in *Time and Narrative,* vol. 3, Kathleen McLaughlin and David Pellauer, trans. (Chicago: University of Chicago Press, 1988), 116–26.

12 Lowenthal, *The Past is a Foreign Country,* 185.

13 Ibid., 186.

14 Ibid., 239.

15 Ibid., 248.

16 Iain Sinclair, *Lights Out For The Territory* (London: Granta Books, 1997), 1.

17 Rainer Maria Rilke, *The Notebooks of Malte Laurids Brigge,* Stephen Mitchell, trans. (New York: Vintage Books, 1985), 46–47.

18 Antoni Tàpies, quoted adjacent to a work by Tàpies in the Scottish National Gallery of Modern Art, Edinburgh, Scotland.

19 Ricoeur, *Time and Narrative,* vol. 3, 125.

20 Edward S. Casey, *Remembering: A Phenomenological Study* (Bloomington: Indiana University Press, 1987), 90.

21 Pierre Nora, "Between Memory and History: *Les Lieux du Mémoire*," *Representations* 26 (Spring 1989), 7.

22 Ibid., 19.

23 Ibid.

24 Ibid., 13.

25 Ibid.

26 See Walter J. Ong, *Orality and Literacy: The Technologizing of the Word* (London: Routledge, 1988).

27 Nora, "Between Memory and History," 9.

28 See Pope, *Ladders*.

29 Mohsen Mostafavi and David Leatherbarrow, *On Weathering: The Life of Buildings in Time* (Cambridge, MA: MIT Press, 1993), 84–86.

30 Scarry, 283.

31 See Halbwachs, *The Collective Memory*, 128–57.

32 Martin Heidegger, "Building Dwelling Thinking," in David F. Krell, ed., *Martin Heidegger: Basic Writings*, Albert Hofstadter, trans. (New York: Harper & Row, 1977), 327.